"*Jesus the Fool* is a unique and refreshing book. Surely the main reason for this is that the Jesus we encounter in Mike's writings is always so surprising, so wonderfully intriguing, and so subversive and challenging. This, combined with the fact that the people of God can never get enough of the central Person of our faith, means that this book will always remain current. One of the great communicators of our age does it again . . . again."

Alan Hirsch, author of *The Forgotten Ways,* co-author of *The Shaping of Things To Come* and *ReJesus*

"Rediscovering the radical, outrageous, and deeply attractive Jesus of the Gospels is essential in a post-Christendom culture that is weary of conventional religion. Michael Frost offers fresh, culturally attuned readings of familiar parables and incidents in the life of Jesus, illustrated with apt contemporary anecdotes and applications, showing how Jesus (as fool, jester, and prophet) overturned conventional wisdom, challenged assumptions, and reframed expectations. *Jesus the Fool* stirs our imagination, disturbs our complacency, and invites us to see God, the world, and ourselves in new ways."

Stuart Murray Williams, author of *Post-Christendom* and founder of Anabaptists Network, UK

"*Jesus the Fool* is as timely today as when it was first released. Michael Frost introduces us to the Jesus that many would not recognize today, yet is the authentic Jesus many are actually looking for, a Jesus that is de-culturalized and de-sanitized."

Darryl Gardiner, national director, New Zealand Youth for Christ

"Christians like Jesus. They like him a lot. So to call a book *Jesus the Fool* might seem risky. But Mike Frost was willing to take risks to get people thinking about Jesus. This book was the first sign of his sustained effort to provoke, disturb, cajole, confuse, charm, persuade, and, if necessary, beg people to open themselves to discovering old truths in new ways."

Glen Powell, Mission Consultant with the Uniting Church, Australia

"Michael Frost's little book reminds me of the King James translation of Hebrews 10:24: 'And let us consider one another to provoke unto love and to good works.' Michael's title and some of his catchphrases are irritating, but they provoke us in the right direction. Jesus clearly broke with conventional wisdom, and there is no way to follow him without appearing foolish to those who choose not to."

John Kaiser, author of *Winning on Purpose*, president, Fellowship of Evangelical Baptist Churches, Canada

"From God's viewpoint, outsiders are in, and insiders are out. The price of following Jesus may be high, and such a life may look foolish, dangerous, and out of control to a society that is its own standard and that believes it walks a safe path in the middle of the road. But the price of NOT following Jesus—and ending up leading a defeated, adapted, purposeless, safe, predictable, and therefore boring life that makes sense to your bank but not to God—is even higher. My motto has always been 'If you dare to do the ridiculous, God will do the impossible.' Now, with this book in print, I even have a sound theology for this. Thanks, Mike!"

Wolfgang Simson, author of *Houses that Change the World* and *The Starfish Manifesto*

MICHAEL FROST

The MISSION of the
UNCONVENTIONAL CHRIST

HENDRICKSON
PUBLISHERS

Jesus the Fool: The Mission of the Unconventional Christ

© 2010 by Hendrickson Publishers Marketing, LLC
P. O. Box 3473
Peabody, Massachusetts 01961-3473

ISBN 978-1-59856-358-0

A shorter, earlier version of this book was published as *Jesus the Fool,* by Michael Frost, Albatross Books, Australia, 1994.

Printed in the United States of America

First Printing — April 2010

This book was printed with a FSC (Forest Stewardship Council) chain-of-custody certified printer. Highest environmental and social standards are applied to forest conservation, responsible management, and community level benefits for people near the forests that provide this paper and in the printing facilities that turned the paper into this book. The cover is 100% PCW recycled stock, and the text is printed on 30% post consumer waste paper, using only soy or vegetable content inks.

Library of Congress Cataloging-in-Publication Data

Frost, Michael, 1961–
    Jesus the fool : the mission of the unconventional Christ / Michael Frost.
        p. cm.
    Includes bibliographical references (p.   ).
    ISBN 978-1-59856-358-0 (alk. paper)
        1. Jesus Christ—Person and offices—Biblical teaching. 2. Bible. N.T. Luke—Criticism, interpretation, etc. 3. Fools and jesters—Religious aspects—Christianity. 4. Folly—Religious aspects—Christianity. I. Title.
    BT205.F76 2010
    226.4′064—dc22
                  2010004513

To John Waterhouse, a Christ-like fool who has inspired me by his laughable contempt for conventional wisdom and who cocked his ear in my direction before anyone else was listening.

CONTENTS

FOREWORD

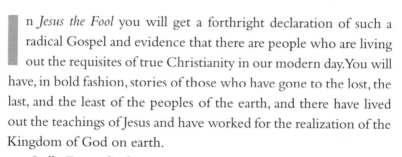

I n *Jesus the Fool* you will get a forthright declaration of such a radical Gospel and evidence that there are people who are living out the requisites of true Christianity in our modern day. You will have, in bold fashion, stories of those who have gone to the lost, the last, and the least of the peoples of the earth, and there have lived out the teachings of Jesus and have worked for the realization of the Kingdom of God on earth.

Sadly, Evangelicalism, instead of being defined by those outside the Church as a compassionate movement, committed to living out love on the personal level and justice on the social level, has earned the reputation of being anti-gay; anti-environmentalism; anti-women; pro-war and power hungry triumphalism. Most people in secular society have a great respect for Jesus, but see little similarity between what He was and taught and what is expressed in contemporary Evangelical Christendom.

Living, as I do, in the United States, I am especially aware of the negative connotations that go with the word Evangelical. This is so much the case that many of us have begun to abandon the name with all of its connotations. Older Christians such as Jim Wallis, Ron Sider and myself, along with the younger generation of Christian leaders such as Brian McLaren and Shane Claiborne, have adopted a new name. We call ourselves Red Letter Christians. We like this designation because most Christians know that "red letters" refers to those passages of the Bible that denote words that Christ Himself uttered. On the other hand, the secular community hasn't a clue as to what the label means. This puts us in a position of having to define it for them and keeps them from defining us without our permission.

Jesus the Fool's Michael Frost would obviously fit in with us Red Letter Christians in that he is seeking an authentic spirituality that adheres uncompromisingly to the message and directives of Jesus Christ. In Him we find a relevant message for our time for He speaks for nonviolence in a world that has gone crazy with war, and He teaches, over and over again, the responsibility of His followers to address the needs of the poor and to alleviate the sufferings of the oppressed. In the Red Letters we find that Jesus comes not only to bring personal salvation but also to make clear that He is initiating a kingdom that will be marked by justice. We contend that all the rest of the Bible (the verses written in black letters) must be read through the eyes of Jesus in order to get their true meaning. What Jesus was, is, and taught provides the lens through which we read Scripture and the lens through which we view society. It is my hope that after you read this book, you will want to join Michael and the rest of us who call ourselves Red Letter Christians to declare a holistic Gospel for the whole world.

There is no question that Jesus came preaching a Kingdom here on earth and prayed for it in His universally known prayer. Such a Kingdom is marked by transformed people living in a transformed society. To negate either of these is to distort the Gospel and be guilty of heresy. In the end, heresy is always a distortion of the truth.

What is required is for individuals to be open to an infusion by the Holy Spirit so that they can be transformed into transformers of society. Such transformed people will have lives marked by personal piety, but they will have much more than that. They will be persons who are willing to sacrifice all that they are and all that they have to live out the call that they have heard from Christ, who told them that unless they deny themselves in serving His Kingdom, they could not be His true disciples.

There is a new movement abroad in the world and you are invited to be a part of it. You will be asked to have a fresh reading of Scripture that will carry you back to its original meaning. It is a Christianity that is politically involved without being partisan. It adheres to no existing political party or organization but speaks in the midst of each of them the words of justice derived from the red letters. It is a Christianity that calls upon all who will listen and join us to realize that we are invited to invade all the structures of the socioeconomic order so as to be the leaven and salt that transforms them, little by little, but very definitely, into what Christ willed for them to be. You are invited to be part of a Church that, in accord with the closing verses of the first chapter of Ephesians, is to be used by Christ to bring all principalities, all powers, all dominions, and all thrones into subjection to His will.

This new movement does not reject the institutional Church as it presently exists and does not ask that its members walk away from it. Instead, we ask those who would be Red Letter Christians to become zealously involved in the institutional churches that dot the landscape, recognizing that institutional churches are themselves principalities and powers that must be permeated with people who are alive with radical Christianity so that they might in turn become a faithful bride of Christ and instruments through which the new Israel can become an existential reality. In this book, you will hear from one of these radical Red Letter Christians who have been crying in the wilderness and *in* now being heard. People, young and old, are recognizing the validity of what is being said and they are saying that we are tired of "playing church" and want to join with others who share a vision of the future that is in harmony with Scripture.

We are people who believe in accord with Philippians 1:9 *1:6* that Christ has begun a good work in us and is working through us. We are convinced that what is accomplished in time and history will be brought to completion when our Lord returns and the kingdoms of this world will become the Kingdom of our God. He shall reign forever and ever. Hallelujah!

We invite you to be part of this incredible revolution and we are sure that once you taste what it is all about you will find the message irresistible, participation joyful and its significance such as to provide ultimate meaning for your life. Read on and as you read get a taste of what it means to become a Red Letter Christian and become one of us.

The fact that Christianity has survived the watering down of its message for almost 2000 years is evidence that it must be ordained of God. The Church has done more to destroy the message of Christ than the arguments of all the atheists and agnostics combined. But it's not too late to set things right. We need to listen to those voices who are crying in the wilderness, calling for a recovery of Biblical Christianity with its requirements for radical discipleship and its demands for social justice.

Tony Campolo, PhD
Eastern University
St. Davids, Pennsylvania, USA

God's ways are so mysterious and unusual that they provoke laughter from human beings. Biblical belief concerns the impossible from a human standpoint— something laughable and ridiculous. In fact, if it can't be laughed about, it can't really be believed at all, since it would fall within the realm of human abilities.
—Joseph Grassi

The prophetic aspect of folly has, throughout the ages, functioned as a form of challenge to the accepted norms, conventions and authorities within society.
—Alastair Campbell

INTRODUCTION: THE CHURCH OF THE HOLY FOOL

andering through the cavernous Museum of Contemporary Art in Bordeaux, France, I came across an exhibition that included the work of the American absurdist artist Reverend Ethan Acres. I'd not heard of Acres before, but I was intrigued by the fact that an ordained minister was exhibiting in an avant-garde exhibition in the south of France.

Wanting to know more, I read the biographical sketch in the exhibition brochure and noted that Acres was not only an artist dedicated to "the expression of religious ecstasy through irrational and absurdist behavior," but was also the minister of the Church of the Holy Fool in Sheffield, Alabama. It turns out that Ethan Acres is renovating an old church building, only a short walk from the historic Muscle Shoals Sound Recording Studio, to become a monastic retreat for artists who live and work in the Deep South.

Now, I've never been to Sheffield, Alabama, but I feel as though I might have visited the Church of the Holy Fool many times in my life. Or at least I've met some bona fide members of that church. I've run into holy fools all over the world, doing absurd things to foster the mission of the unconventional Christ, Jesus.

In Switzerland, I met a bluegrass guitarist who told me his favorite music venue is a cobbler's workshop in Steffisburg, a beautiful village south of Bern. I was intrigued. My picture of a typical Swiss cobbler was anything but cool, but it turns out that Edi Geissler, a devout Christian with a passion for hospitality, has converted his shoemaking workshop into a bistro called Alte Schmitte (the Old Smithy). Geissler hosts concerts, polit-cafés, discussions and various exhibitions, serves food, and has created a popular venue where musicians and patrons revel in the relaxed and creative atmosphere. In the name of Jesus he is breathing life into the village of Steffisburg.

In Brisbane in northern Australia, Peter Breen, a Wesleyan minister, owns a gallery and music venue called Jugglers Art Space. Jugglers was originally an art café, but has developed into an iconic space for street artists and the indie music scene. In addition to having regular exhibitions, Jugglers hosts monthly music sessions and occasional prayer labyrinths. The philosophy behind Jugglers is that "creativity is part of being human and flourishes with positive encouragement." Breen and his son Randall, who manages the space (his other son is a stand-up comedian who performs regularly at Jugglers), are convinced that beauty and creativity don't need to be market-driven to be valid, something only a fool could believe in today's economic climate. Fittingly, their logo is a medieval jester juggling balls.

The village of Andong, just outside Phnom Penh in Cambodia, is comprised of resettled squatters who had been evicted by government forces from the river bank slums in the city. Dumped in a swamp not far from the airport, the evicted squatters struggled to survive, now nearly an hour away from the menial laboring jobs they previously had in Phnom Penh. Then Abraham Hang moved into the slum. A Bible College graduate with a foolish entrepreneurial streak, Hang set about having the swamp drained by digging channels that carried rainwater to a nearby lake. He arranged for Christian doctors and dentists to conduct mobile clinics in the slum, and via an American missionary he has raised the money to build thatched housing for hundreds of families. He has even purchased a truck to ferry workers to and from Phnom Penh each day (public transport costs are greater than a day's wage for an unskilled Cambodian worker). When the local governor saw that the swamp was now inhabitable land he threatened to evict the residents for a second time. It was Abraham who stood up to him, defending his poor community. He has been attacked by the governor's thugs and threatened with various enticements to leave, but he foolishly remains loyal to the vulnerable people to whom God sent him.

Adrian Plass is an English satirist who only took up writing after a painful emotional breakdown. "Angry and upset and fed up with the church," Plass began writing softly satirical novels that picked fun at the excesses and eccentricities of the church in England. He is particularly partial to taking pot-shots at the unquestioned and faddish expressions of sacredness that sweep through the church from time to time. Plass's books go where few Christian authors are prepared to go; they question everything. With no patience for the false pietism of many churchgoers, he observes their behavior as an outsider and continues to ask why. His great skill as a comedic writer relaxes his readers, disarming them, opening them up to the sting of his critique of silly church behavior.

Adrian Plass, Abraham Hang, Peter Breen, Edi Geissler and Ethan Acres are all bona fide members of the church of the holy fool. They thumb their noses at conventional wisdom and find their own way of faithfully following Jesus. In so doing they prove to be the most saintly of fools.

The Saintliness of the Fool

While conventional saints renounce the profane world in order to devote their lives to God through chastity, poverty, and humility, the saintly fools prefer life out in the open in the secular world. They tend to be conspicuously public figures, encountered more readily on the street than in a church or monastery. Their ministry is sometimes mistaken for secular work or seen by the mainstream church community as frivolous or unimportant. Edi Geissler runs a bistro in a shoemaker's workshop. Peter Breen owns an art gallery. And yet it's in their unconventional approach that we can find the seeds of true ministry; the practice of hospitality or the fostering of beauty and creativity. Theirs is a kind of holiness that is demonstrated through engagement with ordinary society, rather than by a retreat from it.

Holy fools intentionally make themselves conspicuous. Since their best work is to provoke an interest in the divine, they look for ways to be surrounded by people hungry for spiritual truth. In fact, in Medieval times many of the holy fools of the Eastern Orthodox Church either spoke in riddles or performed mime for their audiences. Some even had special intermediaries who interpreted their utterances, actions, and silences for curious spectators. So their actions were never taken at face value; instead their listeners looked for hidden or symbolic meanings in their words or behavior. A writer like Adrian Plass epitomizes this approach; his words set off levels of meaning long after they've been read.

The saintly fool consistently defies the rules set by society. While all conventional standards would insist you get out of any slum you were unfortunate enough to end up in, Abraham Hang moves *into* one with his pregnant wife. When the local governor sees an opportunity to evict the slum dwellers of Andong, Abraham resists him with no more force than his saintly foolishness. And so far he has triumphed. The immunity often enjoyed by saintly fools like Abraham adds to their authority among their public and enables them at times to play the role of spokesman. Remember the prophet Nathan's role as the champion of truth in the court of King David. Even the old Tsars of Russia offered their holy fools immunity from punishment and trembled before their rebuke.

This isn't to say saintly fools are always listened to. Plenty of so-called wise ones interpret the saintly fool's behavior as lunacy and treat them as mad and nothing more. And yet in a strange way, a holy fool must, in part, have an audience that is bewildered or angered by his or her words and actions. They challenge their audiences by constantly contravening both social and religious norms, and as a result they can be cruelly beaten or mocked or at best ignored.

An Ancient Tradition

The phenomenology of the holy fool has its roots in the very beginning of the Christian era. In fact, the Apostle Paul was the first apologist of saintly folly, declaring that "the wisdom of this world is foolishness before God" (1 Corinthians 1:19). He continued:

> We are fools for Christ's sake, but you are prudent in Christ; we are weak, but you are strong; you are distinguished, but we are without honor. To this present hour we are both hungry and thirsty, and are poorly clothed, and are roughly treated, and are homeless; and we toil, working with our own hands; when we are reviled, we bless; when we are persecuted, we endure; when we are slandered, we try to conciliate; we have become as the scum of the world, the dregs of all things, even until now (1 Corinthians 4:10–13).

Paul not only coined the term "fool for Christ's sake," he also identified Jesus as the initiator of the holy foolish paradigm. And the Gospel writers seem to agree with him. They present Jesus as a madman (John 10:20) and depict his passion as the sum-composite of humiliation, mockery, derision, and powerlessness (Matthew 27:29–31, 39–42, Mark 15:29–32, Luke 23:35–37). This picture of Jesus the fool and the self-confessed foolishness of the Apostle Paul set in motion a tradition of saintly folly that weaves its way through church history.

In keeping with this tradition, the early church father and master orator John Chrysostom wrote:

> When God reveals something, one has to accept it with faith and not scrutinize it defiantly. . . . Let them call me . . . foolish in Christ and I will be proud of this name as of a victorious crown. Because I

will share this name with Paul. It was he who said: "We are fools for Christ's sake." Such folly is wiser than any wisdom. That foolishness which comes from Christ achieved what mundane wisdom cannot find: it has vanquished the gloom of the Universe, it has brought the light of awareness. What is foolishness according to Christ? [It is] when we harness our musings, which are in a state of inappropriate raving, when we cleanse and liberate our minds of the fruits of [our] mundane upbringing—so that [when] the time comes to listen to Christ's will and testament it would open itself to perceive the Divine words having been freed and well cleansed.

By the fifth century this tradition of holy folly was becoming well entrenched. The great theologian Augustine drew a sharp distinction between the wisdom of God and the wisdom of the world, which he said was incapable of grasping the divine. He refutes such worldly wisdom by defining it as folly:

> They do not know the way by which they should descend from themselves to Him, and by Him ascend to Him. They do not know this way, and they fancy themselves raised on high and shining with the stars, whereas they fall upon the earth and their foolish heart is darkened.

He also offers an apologetic for why the holy fool was obligated to break social laws and prohibitions:

> . . . many actions that to men seem blameworthy, are approved in Your sight; and many that are praised by men are condemned by You, O God—all because often the appearance of the act may be quite different in the situation. But when on a sudden You order something unusual and improbable, even if You had formerly forbidden it, it must obviously be done—though You may conceal the cause of Your demand for the time and though it may be against the ordinance of this or that society of men: a society of men is just, only if it obeys You. But happy are they who know that it was You who commanded.

Augustine denounces human pride because it drives people away from God. He also criticizes an excessive kind of rationalism that denies the precepts of the Christian faith. In this way, without

using such a phrase, he affirms the saintly folly required of all followers of Jesus.

By the Dark Ages, it fell to the "sinner monk" Bernard of Clair-
vaux, to take up the cause of holy foolishness, as the following passage shows:

> I shall play, that I may be mocked. A good game, this, by which Mi-
> chael is enraged and God is pleased. A good game, I say, which is ri-
> diculous to men, but a very beautiful spectacle to the angels (cf. 1 Cor
> 4:9). I say it is a good game by which we become "a reproach to the
> rich and a contempt to the proud" (cf. Ps 122:4).

As mentioned earlier, the holy fools of the Eastern Church during this period were rather more eccentric in their public displays of
folly. But Bernard made the distinction between a sinful jester and
a holy man playing the fool:

> We are like jesters and tumblers, who, with heads down and feet up,
> exhibit extraordinary behavior by standing or walking on their hands,
> and thus draw all eyes to themselves. But ours is not the play of chil-
> dren or of the theatre, which excites lust and represents sordid acts in
> the effeminate and shameful contortions of the actors. No, ours is a
> joyous game, decent, grave, and admirable, delighting the gaze of the
> heavenly onlookers. This chaste and religious game he plays who says:
> "We are made a spectacle to angels and to men" (1 Cor 4:9).

In the thirteenth century, no greater mind than that of Thomas
Aquinas took up the cause of holy folly. He not only distinguished
between the sinful folly of secular wisdom and the divine folly of
unconditional devotion to God but also proclaimed the virtues of
foolishness in Christ:

> One who is strengthened by God professes himself to be an utter fool
> by human standards, because he despises what the wisdom of men
> strives for.

And then again in the sixteenth century, Ignatius of Loyola,
founder of the Society of Jesus, better known as the Jesuits, reclaimed

the red garment of the humiliated Christ. He defined the spiritual orientation of Jesuits in the following way:

> Just as the men of the world, who follow the world, love and seek with great diligence, honors, fame, and esteem for a great name of earth . . . so those who are progressing in the spiritual life and truly following Christ our Lord, love and intensely desire everything opposite. . . . they would wish to suffer injuries, false accusations and affronts, and to be held and esteemed as fools (but without giving any occasion for this); because of their desire to resemble and imitate in some manner our Creator and Lord Jesus Christ, by putting on his clothing and uniform. . . .

But perhaps no one embodied the idea of the holy fool more fully than the saintly Francis of Assisi. This poor little man astounded and inspired the church by taking the Gospel literally, not in a narrow fundamentalist sense, but by actually following all that Jesus said and did, joyfully and without limit. For his trouble he was considered a madman.

After a bout of serious illness, Francis turned to prayer and contemplation and experienced a transformative encounter with Christ during which he felt called to a life of poverty and chastity. He gave up every material thing he had, even piling his clothes before his father (who was demanding restitution for the many gifts Francis had given to the poor). His behavior was seen as so repugnant to his former friends that he was ostracized by his community. When he began begging from door to door for money to continue his work, his town responded with sadness or disgust or outright ridicule.

However, a few people slowly began to realize that Francis was actually trying to follow Jesus. He was taking literally Jesus' command to his disciples to: "Announce the kingdom! Possess no gold or silver or copper in your purses, no traveling bag, no sandals, no staff" (Luke 9:1–3).

When other young men applied to join him, Francis' only rule was a collection of texts from the Gospels. He had no idea of founding an order, other than a foolish resolve to imitate Christ. Like Jesus, he pursued a life of itinerant preaching of the Good News. And even on his deathbed (at the relatively young age of 44) he asked his superior to have his clothes removed when the last hour came and for permission to expire lying naked on the earth, in imitation of his Lord.

Still Foolish Today

The folly commended by the great church fathers and saints is still being lived out today. It can be seen in the brightly colored houses and extravagant gardens created by Father Damian in the leper colony of Molokai in Hawaii. It can be seen in the dour sacrifice of the "red virgin" Simone Weil during World War II. It's clearly seen in the selflessness of Mother Theresa of Calcutta and in the beautifully ridiculous decision of the young English woman, Jackie Pullinger to live in the drug-infested slums of Hong Kong (and to stay there faithfully for 40 years). And such folly is also seen in the serious playfulness of Shane Claiborne from Philadelphia.

Claiborne is a modern day holy fool. After a brief stint with Mother Theresa in Calcutta, and a three-week mission to Baghdad during the American bombardment of that city in 2002, he returned to the US where he established the Simple Way and later the Potter Street Community, a new monastic community that lives among the poor in urban Philadelphia. Noted for foolish stunts like his Baghdad visit, Claiborne would regularly turn up at the scene of gang violence in Philadelphia and begin juggling and clowning to distract the angry mobs that had gathered there. In the concrete jungle of central Philly he has established a community garden and in a world obsessed with fashion and designer labels, he makes his own clothes. Even when in 2007 a fire at the abandoned warehouse across the street destroyed The Simple Way Community Center where Claiborne lived, taking with it all of his possessions, he continued to live out the foolish joy and saintly grace that has epitomized his ministry since his Calcutta days.

Such foolishness seems to abound today. A friend of mine, Ash Barker from Melbourne, after a decade living among the suburban poor of his home town moved into Klong Toey, the largest slum in Thailand, taking his young family with him. There they embody the foolishness of Jesus to the poorest of the world's poor. Inspired by Ash and his wife Anji, another friend, Jon Owen, moved to Mount Druitt, a desperately needy community in western Sydney, indicative of their unconventional wisdom. They have truly been captivated by Jesus the fool, and they have followed him bravely into the lives of the marginalized and the oppressed.

It's my hope that these stories and the greater story of Jesus to which they point will continue to trouble those who prefer benign, conventional, vanilla-flavored Christianity. The fool, Jesus, will continue his work in calling us to take the alternative, unsafe, foolish road, a road already walked by such wise fools as Francis of Assisi, Abraham Hang, Adrian Plass, Flannery O'Connor, Thomas Merton, Henri Nouwen and Shane Claiborne. *Jesus the Fool* attempts to remind us that the way of following Jesus is rarely the safe one. It draws heavily on the work of Alastair Campbell and Kenneth Bailey. Sadly, many people will not have even heard of either, let alone read anything they have written. But I am indebted to both of them for the basic ideas that have given rise to this book.

Some considerable time ago, Alastair Campbell wrote a very influential book called *Rediscovering Pastoral Care*, which tends to be read by pastoral counselors and ministers but not by many others. In it, he includes an excellent chapter called "Wise Fool" in which he explores the style of Jesus and his wise folly as a model for pastoral care. It was upon reading his book, and in particular that chapter, that I began to consider the crazy possibility of Jesus as a fool. This was the seed-thought that has germinated into the work you are about to read.

Better known is Kenneth Bailey, who has written two remarkable books, *Poet and Peasant* and *Through Peasant Eyes*, both of which seek to rediscover the original intent behind many of Jesus' parables, drawing on Bailey's own experience as a missionary in the Middle East. He will be recognized by some as the author of *The Cross and the Prodigal*, but unfortunately neither of these other two books has been readily accessible to the average reader. They explore at great length the structure and pattern within each parable and thereby assume a pretty high level of theological and biblical familiarity. And yet I have never been more impacted by the theology of Jesus than I was after reading Bailey's work.

In my small way, I have attempted to synthesize Campbell's idea of the wise fool and Bailey's interpretations of the parables in such a way as to make their separate and yet complementary views of Jesus more accessible. I trust that, like the two lenses of a pair of binoculars, their insights might form a clearer picture of Jesus for you, as they have for me.

WILL THE REAL JESUS PLEASE STAND UP!

I've got a picture of Jesus,
In his arms so many prayers rest.
We've got a picture of Jesus,
And with him we shall be forever blessed.
—Ben Harper

Jesus was a fool. This statement will not sit too comfortably with some, but I need some licence to explain myself. As you've already opened the first page of this book, the chances are you are prepared to give me some leeway, and I appreciate that. In my previous book about Jesus, *ReJesus,* Alan Hirsch and I referred to him as a wild Messiah, so it might seem surprising that I now refer to him as a fool, but when I do so, I don't mean what you may expect. Perhaps you will take my word for that until I can explain.

New pictures of Jesus

My concern here is to develop new ways of picturing Jesus, new expressions of his life and work, new imaginings of his mission and his impact on his own culture and ours. Now when I say "new pictures" or "new expressions," I don't mean that we recreate him as though he was some plasticine model that can be plied into a myriad of shapes to suit our own particular perspectives. Far from it.

In fact, I probably don't mean "new" at all. Rather, I think we ought to rediscover the original Jesus as presented by his chroniclers in the Gospels. And there we will find perspectives that are so surprising that we might well think of them as "new" and innovative.

I know Jesus as a fool is a surprising perspective, but no matter how surprising, we find him playing the fool again and again in the Gospels (which, despite the kerfuffle caused by *The Da Vinci Code*, really are the best kept secrets in Christianity). It's just that we have become used to certain legendary qualities of Jesus: one who is invariably austere, mystical, aloof—almost spooky. He never seems real. And as such he frightens or repels us, rather than wooing and winning us. I have explored this with Alan Hirsch in *ReJesus*. Jesus invites us to follow him, not just worship him. I want to suggest that we have moved too far from the biblical information regarding Jesus and have lost touch with the real man. Jesus was a fool, a wild fool. And it is as the fool that he is at his most intriguing.

The Hollywood Jesus

I remember as a boy seeing a movie about the life of Christ. One scene in it had a profound impact on me—in fact, it haunted me for some time. It was a standard Hollywood treatment of Jesus' life and ministry (I think it was directed by Zeferelli and featured a galaxy of American movie stars) and, true to form, portrayed him as a vacant-eyed weirdo traveling about Palestine teaching about love and some strange Christ-consciousness.

But one scene knocked me off my feet. In this scene, Jesus and his disciples were playing some ancient game with a stone. They would throw the stone to each other, then pummel the person caught holding it too long. At school we used a ball and called this game kill-the-dill-with-the-pill. In the film, Jesus was the one caught with the rock, and he became the target of his friends who all threw themselves on the hapless Messiah.

As they climbed off him, to their horror, they found him motionless, his eyes closed, his face expressionless. A gasp of terror. We've killed him, they thought. Just as panic began to set in, Jesus flicked open his eyes and roared with laughter. It was a trick—and everyone enjoyed the joke. Everyone except me, watching at home one Saturday afternoon (probably around Eastertime when the networks always schedule these movies). It bothered me a great deal as I wrestled with the great theological dilemma as to whether or not Jesus would actually play tricks on his friends. As I said, it was a pretty daring scene in what was otherwise a typically conservative portrayal of the life of Jesus.

What this did was to confront my personal picture of Jesus and force me to consider whether or not I could make it fit. A statement like "Jesus was a fool" confronts us with the same dilemma. It doesn't fit into our accepted pictures of him. I had not had a very religious upbringing at all and therefore had a pretty vague image of this man called Jesus of Nazareth. The primary source of my religious insight came from the white leather-bound Bible my mother kept in the drawer of her bedside table.

My mother had come from traditional working-class Irish Catholic stock and had been presented with the Bible at her first Holy Communion. While she had been very devout in her faith as a younger woman (she had considered but rejected the decision to become a nun, something for which I will always be grateful), by the time I was old enough to show interest in the book it had long lain undisturbed in the drawer. It was a powerfully mysterious volume to me. The pages were so thin as to be almost transparent, and the leather cover, due to neglect, had grown brittle and was cracking at the edges. I don't know where or when I first heard that this was God's book, but I recall always having the sense that there was something holy about it. The type was so tiny, the language so outdated and the font so flowery that I honestly believed it was written in an indecipherable speech, God's own language. It was filled with illustrated plates depicting scenes from various Bible stories: there was Daniel in the lions' den; Ruth and Naomi on the road to Palestine; Joseph and his colored coat. And then there was, as the frontispiece, a commanding picture of Jesus, the good shepherd.

This picture of Jesus became my sole religious instructor. It depicted him as a gentle, caring, nurturing, loving shepherd. He had long, neatly parted ash-blonde hair, curled carefully at his collar. His beard was clipped about his strong, square jaw, and his eyes were piercing and icy blue. A quiet gentleness beamed from his face. In fact, there was something strangely feminine about him. He stood at the edge of a craggy cliff face. About him storm clouds gathered, and there was a foreboding darkness about the place. But he was alight, his long flowing robe dashing in the wind. With one hand clasping his shepherd's crook, he reached with the other down to a stranded lamb, caught at the precipice.

For many years I loved to imagine myself as the rescued lamb. I have no idea what I expected to be rescued from, but the sense of care and nurture flooded over me as I examined the picture at great length. The picture had convinced me that Jesus was earnest, decisive, competent—that he was on a quest with no time for the trivialities of life. He was reliable and dependable, but not quite human. He was an androgynous heavenly being who performed his missions of rescue and moved on to his next calling. He was not unlike another hero of mine at the time, the Lone Ranger, whose well known line, "It looks like our work here is finished, Tonto" always signaled the end of another adventure. So you can imagine why the idea of this immaculate cosmic shepherd playing kill-the-dill-with-the-pill disturbed me so much. It forced a radical reassessment that has been taking place to this day.

My desire is to fuel a similar reassessment in the lives of those I encounter. Too many people have written Jesus off as some soft guru, a man with a perpetual smile on his face who wandered around Palestine kissing babies and patting happy children on the head. He has been portrayed as having modelled an unflappable equanimity that seems more mellow-yellow than genuinely spiritual.

The Gospel picture of Jesus

But the Jesus we meet in the Gospels is quite different than the one we encounter in films or, dare I say it, in the preaching from many pulpits around the Christian world. Of course, looking to the Gospels for Jesus presumes some confidence in the Gospels themselves. Some people suggest they weren't even written by the contemporaries of Jesus. Even the most conservative Christians acknowledge that Mark and Luke were recording events second-hand. Why, all four Gospels were written several decades after Jesus' death. So how reliable are they?

Some skeptics believe that in their desire to promote faith in Jesus, the Gospel writers were inclined to myth-making and embellishment. With such a motive, you would expect they would have presented a very impressive, almost unreal picture of him. If the Gospel writers were into perpetuating the embellished memory of a dead rabbi (in much the same way that Elvis still lives according to many "experts" in America), you would expect that they would portray him in a way that befitted a great religious leader of superior, godly qualities. Not so. Rather, they depicted Jesus as a remarkably human and multifaceted man. The reality of the man, Jesus, couldn't possibly have been made up by those wanting to develop some cult of personality around him.

The Gospels show him to be a man who was continually frustrated, occasionally angry, a man who was at times scared, sad, and dreadfully lonely. He is presented with such a refreshing and honest realism they could not have made him up! The Gospel writers were hardly the priests of a new cultus; rather, they were accurate reporters, dedicated to the presentation of the facts surrounding this strange and wonderful man who had so thoroughly transformed their lives.

One such reporter was Luke. He, in an attempt to make some sense and order out of all the tales and anecdotes he had gathered concerning Jesus, has strung them together in a kind of spiritual travel narrative. He tells the story of Jesus and his community of followers hitting the road, bound for Jerusalem and, as they make their way, having a series of adventures and encounters. It is not dissimilar to the style employed by John Bunyan in his mammoth allegory, *Pilgrim's Progress*. *The Wizard of Oz* is another example. The journey becomes the crucible into which the details of the story are poured. It is Luke who most peculiarly portrays Jesus as the fool—as the traveling troubadour bound for tragedy and destruction and yet charting a new and dynamic way of living.

Being drawn to Jesus

To follow Jesus is to embark on this daring journey, to hit the road with the fool. But who will be so daring, who will take such a risk unless Jesus is worth following?

The dramatic color plate in my mother's First Holy Communion Bible depicted a man I would not dare follow, for, while I yearned to be rescued by him (like the lamb in the picture), I was also terrified by him in so many ways. And in keeping with such a picture of Jesus, much preaching in churches concerns a Jesus who frightens and repels rather than draws us to him. In Luke's Gospel, Jesus is clearly a man worth traveling with, a companion who made the journey worth the effort. The Jesus we meet in churches sometimes repels us, not because he is repulsive, but because he is other-worldly. He seems too much like the androgynous, shining, cosmic shepherd I knew for so many years.

It's worth noting the difference between fear and awe. We know fear to be terrifying and repulsive. Fear drives us away. It creates anxiety and thereby it limits, retards, paralyses, and destroys. I don't think this is how we are to approach Jesus. What the Bible means when speaking about the fear of God (and similar phrases) is best translated by our English word "awe." To hold something in awe is quite different than being afraid of it. Fear repels, but awe attracts.

When the Bible anticipates that we will hold God in awe, it expects that we will be drawn to him. Not too close. The Hebrews and early Christians held him in very high regard, but he was also the God who said gently, "I will draw you with loving-kindness" (Jeremiah 31:3). We do God and his agent of grace, Jesus, a great disservice when we tell people to fear him without explaining what we mean. And so we need more accurate pictures of Jesus, pictures that express the awe with which his own companions held him as strange, inexplicable, attractive, wonderful man.

One of my favorite cartoonists/satirists is the American illustrator, Ron Cobb (a man not noted for his kindness to the established church). In one of his better-known cartoons he has depicted three men sitting as contestants in a game show. Each of them is bearded and long-haired. The first is neatly coiffed and his beard trimmed. He sits tall and elegantly. He looks remarkably like the man in my mother's Bible. A plaque before him says "Protestant." The second man is bloodied and beaten. His eyes are dark and sunken. From the crown of thorns jammed on his head there are tracks of dried blood. The plaque in front of him says "Catholic." And the third is unkempt and filthy. He is short and ugly and has a large bulbous nose. His eyes are shifty and beady. He looks like a mean, Palestinian thug. His plaque reads "Historical." The caption below the cartoon says, in bold print, "WILL THE REAL JESUS PLEASE STAND UP!"

Rediscovering the Gospel pictures of Jesus

There is a now-legendary story about the Spanish artist Bartholomew Murillo. As a young boy he already showed considerable promise in the visual arts, but was yet to find a patron or any real source of encouragement. In the home where he grew up there was a picture of Jesus hanging in the living area. It was Jesus the shepherd boy and it portrayed him, in the style of the time, standing straight and tall, his shepherd's crook like a sentinel's bayonet. About his head hung the obligatory halo. Murillo detested the picture. So, one day when his family was out of the house, he impetuously took the framed painting down from the wall and went to work on it. His youthful brilliance already evident, he was able to recreate it into a new picture of Christ.

Upon their return home, the Murillos were aghast to see their Lord had been transformed. The stern unflinching face now a lively grin. His eyes were alive with mischief. The halo had become a battered straw hat and the plastered-down hair had become tousled and unruly. His crook had been transformed into a gnarled walking-stick and the limp and sad-looking lamb at Jesus' feet was now a troublesome puppy. The shepherd boy had become a lively and excited hiker in search of adventure.

Apparently, young Bartholomew came to within an inch of losing his life. When the Murillos showed the desecrated picture of their Lord to their friends and neighbors, as if to illustrate the trials they were enduring to a difficult son, a local artist spied the boy's burgeoning talent and offered himself as Bartholomew's patron. And the rest, as they say, is history!

Will the real Jesus please stand up? Sadly, he has been standing now, quite visible, for nearly two thousand years. And yet I suspect that most of us are carrying a picture of Jesus that resembles the first painting in the Murillos' home rather than the second. And there are reasons for this.

The first is that the Gospels do recount a great volume of very serious material about Jesus. The second is that, in the mists of time, we have lost the insight necessary to see the great humor and comedy of the life of Jesus. Things that would have been quite hilarious, or even mildly amusing, to Jesus' contemporaries are taken all so very gravely today. Let me explain a little further about these two reasons for not seeing the more lively, comical aspects of Jesus' life and work. The Gospels are a collection of stories and anecdotes that were recounted orally for decades before they were ever written down. When each of the final authors came to compile this material, several concerns bothered them. There was the order of events to consider. There was the degree to which certain episodes and sayings suited the theological focus of each writer. And there was the simple, yet painful concern of space. This it seems is the editor's eternal dilemma. And it was equally so for the writers of the Gospels. Given the cost of parchment and the mammoth exercise of copying out the text by long hand, the Gospel writer was forced to be decisive.

For instance, John writes in his Gospel: "Jesus did many other things as well. If every one of them were written down, I suppose that even the whole world would not have room for the books that would be written" (John 21:25). John's point is that he had to be selective when compiling his book. And, of course, you can imagine that priority was given to the more significant events, teaching, parables, miracles, and the tragedies of his torture and death. All very serious and sombre stuff. For this reason you won't find Jesus playing kill-the-dill-with-the-pill in Matthew, Mark, Luke, or John.

However, this is not to suggest that comic events and sayings don't make it into the text. As I said, Luke's Gospel is in many respects quite witty. The problem is that we miss the humor because of cultural distance from first-century Palestine. We need to work a little harder and dig a little deeper to find the original intent or original setting. Though not too deep. It is quite clear even to untrained eye. We just need to peel back some of our preconceptions and be prepared to see cherished passages and stories in a different light to the way our Sunday school teachers told us about them. If the real Jesus is to stand up we must let him do so, rather than leave him bound by our religious heritage and misconceptions.

M. Scott Peck, in his book *Further Along the Road Less Traveled,* records Baptist theologian Harvey Cox's retelling of the story of Jesus raising a Jewish leader's daughter from the dead (Luke 8:40–56). As Jesus and his companions are heading for the home of the dying girl, a woman who has been hemorrhaging for years breaks from the crowd and touches his robe in the hope that she too will be healed.

Jesus reels around and demands to know who touched him. The cowering woman owns up, and Jesus, feeling compassionate for her having endured years of unspeakable suffering, heals her and continues on his way to the house where the young girl has since died.

Having related his story (no doubt in greater detail than I just did), Cox asked his audience of six hundred Christian healers and therapists with whom they most identified. The bleeding woman? The anxious father? The curious crowd? Or Jesus? What Cox found was that around a hundred felt they could relate to the desperate woman; several hundred identified with the father whose daughter was dying; the majority identified with the perplexed group standing by. And six—yes, six—people felt they could identify with Jesus.

Peck's point in recounting this experience is that there is something seriously wrong with Christianity when only one in every hundred Christians can identify with Jesus. Have we made Jesus so divine, so other-worldly that we cannot connect with him anymore? He suggests that this leads to the excuse that we can't really be expected to follow Jesus because we perceive ourselves way down here and Jesus way up there, beyond identification. Says Scott Peck:

> That is exactly what we're supposed to do! We're supposed to identify with Jesus, act like Jesus, be like Jesus. That is what Christianity is supposed to be about: the imitation of Christ.[1]

Our pictures of Jesus need some adjusting to correct the over-emphasis on Jesus the divine. He was also human, and exquisitely human at that. And, as human, he is a great source of inspiration and encouragement to us. He is, in fact, very much worth imitating.

Two images of Jesus

In an article on drawing more appropriate pictures of Jesus, Alan Collins, a minister and author from Melbourne, suggests that the deadly serious images that many ministers carry of their Lord contribute in no small way to the very earnest and detached style of ministry they perform. He suggests that if we have a picture of the overly responsible "man for others" (a very common understanding of Jesus), then those of us who are ministers behave in a similar fashion (and ultimately burn out). His suggestion is that if we can draw more accurate pictures of Jesus, we might better embrace the lively, robust approach to life he modelled.

Collins offers his own favorite picture of Jesus. He imagines the tranquil Sea of Galilee, based on postcards he has seen. And there by the glassy, undisturbed water, standing on the pebbly, rocky foreshore, is Jesus. And what is he doing? He's skimming stones across the water's surface, trying to better his previous score with each throw. You might not be surprised to learn that this scene is not recorded by any of the writers of the New Testament. It is pure fantasy. But for Alan Collins, it is an image that reminds him of the humanity of Jesus and his sense of fun and the frivolous.

One of my favorite images of Jesus is, in fact, found in the Gospels. It is also set by the idyllic Sea of Galilee. Here gathering for respite is the small community of believers who had traveled with Jesus and had been shattered when he was destroyed by the religious and civil authorities in Jerusalem. And yet this is not a wake, for the man they once were mourning is now with them again. Yes, the risen, alive-again Jesus is with them. And what is he doing? Glowing in heavenly splendour? Teaching on the secrets of life and death? No, he's just frying fish for breakfast.

Can you imagine it? The sea lapping on the stones. The smell of frying fish sizzling in the pan. And there is Jesus, the God-man who has conquered death and will transform the world, whipping up breakfast for the team. This for me makes the resurrection all the more potent. After he has risen, Jesus doesn't float around the place like some poltergeist, glowing in an otherworldly hue. No, he can squat by a small wood fire with the sea breeze whispering around him and fry fish for breakfast!

Broadening our picture of Jesus

This book aims to do what that dastardly child Bartholomew Murillo did to his parents' favorite picture of Jesus. It is not about defacing much-loved visions of Christ. Far from it. Rather, it seeks to be about broadening our picture to include the vital, lively, mischievous, dynamic, *energetic* way in which Jesus lived life and took a small band of men and women on a journey they would never forget. Jesus had a superb sense of humor. It was earthy, robust, and provocative. I have no doubt that he would have been great fun.

In a film written by Neil Simon, *Biloxi Blues*, based on the author's days in the army as a young man, the unorthodox and infuriating sergeant offers the young soldier a piece of advice as they part company. "Never," he cautions the boy, "underestimate the power of eccentricity." Clearly, that power was at work during the long journey to Jerusalem taken by Jesus and his company. I myself remember my interminable days in teachers' college learning one valuable lesson (I'm sure there was more than one, but none of the others come readily to mind): when predictability is high, the degree of communication that takes place is invariably low. Alternatively, as predictability decreases, so communication increases. The more unpredictable, unorthodox, surprising the communicator, the better he or she communicates. If an audience thinks it knows what you're about to say and you go ahead and say it, they will switch off. But if they're pretty sure they know what's coming next and you turn on them with a surprising application or a shocking illustration, they will be chastened into ever-increasing levels of understanding.

This is Jesus at his best. This is Jesus the fool. Recently, I asked the members of the congregation in the church where I was working to close their eyes and to picture Jesus. I had previously mentioned some of the things I have written here and I wanted them, like Bartholomew Murillo, to draw their own images of Jesus. I also pointed out that any picture that is not in keeping with what we know of Jesus in the Bible is not a legitimate image. I allowed a considerable period of silence before closing the meditation. I must admit I had not intended to ask for verbal responses, but curiosity got the better of me and I invited anyone who wished to share their picture of Jesus with the congregation to do so. Their pictures were surprising but delightful.

One young man imagined himself arriving at the room where Jesus was having the Last Supper. At first, he felt conspicuous and wanted to leave, but he noticed Jesus looking up and his face beaming as he noticed the intruder. His eyes lit up and he was so welcoming that the young intruder felt like a long lost son returning to his father after a long absence. Here was Jesus the father-like figure, offering warmth and acceptance.

A middle-aged woman thought Jesus looked physically disabled. And yet she found him intoxicatingly beautiful. Whilst there was nothing externally attractive about him, he had an irresistible inner beauty. She compared him with the cerebral palsied painter played by Daniel Day-Lewis in the Irish film, *My Left Foot*. When she looked at him, she felt worried that he would not be able to meet her needs and yet, so irresistible was his beauty, she dared not reject him. Here was Jesus for whom attraction and sexuality were not blurred.

Another young man saw himself rap-dancing on stage and Jesus was the only member of the audience. He was black with a flat top hairstyle. He looked a bit like the early rapper, MC Hammer. He kept repeating, "Yo man, that's cool!" over and over. Here was Jesus the affirming, supportive friend.

Will the real Jesus please stand up? Which of the above images is right and which is wrong? Is Jesus not accepting? Is he not attractive? Is he not affirming? Of course, he is all three. For each of those people at that stage in their lives, the real Jesus was very much a part of their consciousness. And no doubt he will change for them at future stages. I hasten to remind you again, Jesus cannot be molded into whatever shape we wish. We are kept in check by the Gospels themselves. We cannot picture Jesus in a way that contradicts the man revealed in Scripture. But my point is that we have done exactly this when we carry with us images of the hyper-religious Jesus. A rediscovery of the biblical Jesus will free us to imagine him more accurately and to find pictures that do him greater justice. These pictures can be incredibly helpful. So let us not be afraid to encounter a different picture of Jesus to the one we found in our childhood. I think you'll be surprised by what you find in the Gospels.

"HERE IS A GLUTTON AND A DRUNKARD"

Some people think it is difficult to
be a Christian and to laugh, but I
think it's the other way around. God
writes a lot of comedy, it's just
that he has so many bad actors.
—Garrison Keillor

There is a lot of evidence in the Gospels to suggest that Jesus wasn't taken very seriously in the early part of his public life. That was because he was so unlike anything that the people of first-century Palestine ever expected in a prophet.

Those crazy Jewish prophets

Prophets in Israel were traditionally fierce, fiery, wild men of God. They shunned the materialism and godlessness of their particular culture and affirmed with great force a return to the original ideals of Israel. They were generally ascetic, austere, and fundamentalist. Jesus, however, was none of these things. Consider some of the crazy behavior of the better-known prophets. Hosea married a prostitute and gave her children very ominous names. Isaiah went naked to illustrate Egypt's impending shame.

And Ezekiel? In another time and place they might have locked
him up. He enacted the siege of Jerusalem by drawing a map of
the city on a clay tablet, then building ramps and setting up enemy
camps around it and pounding it with battering rams. His extraordinary, eccentric behavior was to symbolise the Lord's judgment
on Israel. He lay on his left side for 390 days to demonstrate how
he was prepared to bear the sin of Israel—one day for every year of
their rebellion. After that he did the same for the sin of the southern
nation of Judah—another forty days on his right side!

Can you imagine the impact of this amazing pantomime? This
grown man was playing with toy soldiers and battering rams, posi-
tioning the attack, building the approach ramps, preparing for the
sacking of the city and the slaughter of the inhabitants. He lay pros-
trate beside the model for a total of 430 days. That's about fourteen
months. You couldn't be blamed for thinking he was as nutty as a
fruit cake—and no doubt many of his contemporaries did. Some
modern biblical scholars have certainly thought him more than a
little weird.

In 1877 H. Klostermann, a German theologian, suggested, on
the basis of passages such as the one in Ezekiel chapter 3 where the
prophet says "I fell face down" (verse 23) and then God says, "they
will tie you with ropes so that you cannot go among the people"
(verse 25) and "I will make your tongue stick to the roof of your
mouth so that you will be silent" (verse 26), that Ezekiel suffered
from an organic nervous disease, which Klostermann called catalepsy.
It was a pretty popular theory for a while there, but few scholars
hold to it today. Nevertheless, it points out just how strange was
some of his behavior. Ezekiel was an extraordinary man—a vision-
ary, imaginative man of symbolism who appreciated the power of
allegory. He was a sobering, ascetic madman. And I mean that in
the nicest possible way!

So these were the models, the antecedents, that the people in
Jesus' time would have expected. Now the prophets were not neces-

sarily esteemed in their own day. In fact, they were very often reviled and humiliated. Their message was usually ignored because they spoke hard truths and refused to pander to the sensibilities of the people of their time. This does not make for popular communicators.

Very few prophets were as scorned and mocked as the hapless melancholic called Jeremiah. At a time in history when forces of the great conqueror Babylon were like a cauldron about to pour its scalding contents on Judah, Jeremiah used the impending danger as a motivation for repentance. "Return to the Lord and be spared," he cried. At first, he was reviled because of his youth. Called by God as his mouthpiece at a very young age, Jeremiah was ignored for his perceived inexperience. His skill as a communicator, however, was clear. He smashed clay pots. He used rotten loin cloths to illustrate Judah's uselessness. He bought a field as sermon illustration. He refused to marry. He ranted and he raved. And none of his message was good news.

For Jeremiah's trouble he was put in the stocks where, bound hand and foot, he continued to preach. The people threw him into the cavernous underground cisterns to shut him up. But he kept on preaching. Old childhood friends from his home town of Anathoth plotted to murder him because of the shame he was bringing on their school name. And it was at this point he falters.

Abandoned and destitute, he questions his commitment to the cause (and by doing so becomes an inspiration to anyone called to uphold useless causes). But on he presses. Filled with doubt and disillusionment he charges ever onward. Eventually he is banned from his pulpit, the temple in Jerusalem. Unable to preach, he writes down his message and then, on one glorious day, within earshot of the people, the rulers and king Jehoiakim, he reads the manuscript aloud. In response, Jehoiakim has Jeremiah's manifesto—his life's work—unceremoniously burnt before his very eyes.

You might consider giving up at this point. But not Jeremiah. He rewrites the text. He goes on preaching. And when the white-hot fury of the Babylonian army scorches Judah and Israel, Jeremiah is fully vindicated. And this is his ultimate humiliation. He can only be vindicated by watching his nation and his people obliterated by the conquering army.

So these are the men, this was the heritage, the legacy of the "crazy prophets" of Israel and Judah. They were stern fundamentalists (in the sense they were calling their people back to the fundamentals of their faith). They were austere, frightening, uncompromising. Their crazy behavior was seen as madness by those who were too set in their ways to hear God's prophet. The irony of the situation is that although they were considered contemptible in their day, centuries later they had become heroes.

It is not unlike the American attitude to Abraham Lincoln. In his day, he was considered by many an indecisive monster, responsible for the destruction of the unity of the United States through the bitter conflict of the American Civil War. Lincoln was openly referred to as "the Baboon" by his general, George McClelland, and laughed at for his haggard, emaciated features (he suffered from a wasting disease that would have proved fatal even if he had not been assassinated). His famous Gettysburg Address was considered lightweight by the press of the day, since it lasted just over three minutes. But today, he is considered the consummate American statesman, and all subsequent presidents have been judged against his impeccable standard. It has been said that his single greatest and single worst contribution to American life was to raise the expected standard of leadership to unattainable heights. But they weren't saying that in 1861.

Similarly, the Old Testament prophets who had been ignored at best and reviled at worst during their public lives had become the expected standard for all pretenders to the mantle of "prophet of God." And Jesus just didn't fit that mold. To make matters worse, shortly before Jesus began his public ministry two extraordinary men had risen up who *did* meet everyone's long-held expectations.

One, strictly speaking, wasn't a prophet. The other most certainly was. And what's worse, this latter one was Jesus' own cousin.

The long shadow of Judas Maccabeus

The first of these public figures was a Jewish hero called Judas Maccabeus. Since many in Israel were looking for the prophet/savior they called the Messiah, Judas more than many others contributed to the nation's expectations regarding what this Messiah would look like. And so, while certainly not a prophet, as a military leader, a savior and hero of the faith, Judas swelled the people's already unreal expectation. His story is a bloody tale of rebellion and insurrection. And yet he must be considered to be one of the truly great leaders in Israel's history.

After the phenomenally rapid conquests of Alexander the Great, the Greek empire found itself stretched just about half way around the known world. The process by which it contained so heterogeneous and fractured a bevy of cultures is known today as hellenization. This was a program of saturating their vassal states with the Greek culture so as to rob them of their identity and thereby make them less rebellious. It was an ingenious ploy and it worked like magic. Today, we might call it the boiling frog routine.

You know how to boil a frog, don't you? If you throw a live frog into a pot of boiling water, he will jump straight back out again. But if you place him in a pot of cool water and slowly apply the heat, he will sit there and allow himself to be boiled to death. Charming illustration, isn't it? But this is exactly what the Greeks did through hellenization. They introduced the Greek language, customs, pastimes, innovations, and entertainments and slowly converted the vassal nations. In a sense, they seduced them rather than raping them. Another charming illustration.

In Israel, the process of hellenization was a dazzling success. Young Hebrew men began speaking in the supposedly more cultured

Greek language. They dressed in togas and went to the gymnasium to attend naked wrestling matches. Slowly the distinctive elements of Hebrew culture were abandoned. One of these practices was the upholding of the religion of Moses. Never before had Judaism been in such danger of extinction. It had overcome the incursions of the fertility religion of the indigenous Canaanite inhabitants of Israel. It had rejected the Babylonian and Persian tribal desires to which it had been exposed in the four-hundred-year exile. But the Greek strategy was insidiously clever. The Jewish religion was not stamped out or forbidden by the Greeks. It was being gradually abandoned as old-fashioned and useless. Those zealous few who maintained the faith (mainly the Hasidim) were left in peace as being an irrelevant throwback from another era.

The young Alexander died on the battlefield and his successors struggled to keep the mammoth empire in shape. One of these was the maniacal Seleucid monarch, Antiochus IV. He saw in Israel a Judaism that was a pale imitation of what Moses had originally perceived that was rotten to the core. And its worse enemies were within its own ranks. This, of course, was the desired outcome of the process of hellenization: death by atrophy. But Antiochus, a typical oriental despot, was to make a great mistake that was to revitalise and restore Judaism in a way that could have barely happened from within. By deciding to crush temple worship and wipe out Judaism as a whole, he saved it from destruction. In effect, he dropped the frog into boiling water and it jumped back at him.

It is understandable that he thought Judaism was already dead. He might have thought he was landing the final blow to an already lifeless entity. But when he declared himself the incarnation of the god Zeus and decided to abolish all Mosaic ceremonial observance and compel the Jews to worship him in a unified Greek culture, he set in motion a series of events that were to backfire on him. The extremity of his actions saved the historic faith by arousing a frenzy of religious zeal in a family called the Maccabees, who were to prevail against enormous odds and save the Jewish nation. But it took a bloodbath for them to achieve it.

In 167 B.C., Antiochus made an ill-fated move. The Jews were ordered to make unclean sacrifices on the altars of idols and to eat swine's flesh. Then the temple of Jerusalem became the place of worship of the Olympian god, Zeus, which was consecrated with an offering of pork. Furthermore, every village in Palestine was ordered to make similar sacrifices.

Nothing could be expected to raise the ire of the Jews more than this. It was in the small backwater town of Modien, fifteen miles from the capital (not in Jerusalem, the center of Mosaic ritual), that an eruption took place that was to drive the Seleucids from Palestine. There the government legate, carrying out the orders of Antiochus, demanded that the aged priest, Mattathias, complete the defiled sacrifice. The old man refused. And when another Jew stepped forward to comply, Mattathias killed the Jew and the legate, smashed the altar, and took to the hills with his five sons. The Maccabees waged guerrilla warfare on their oppressors for the next twenty years.

The fiery old priest Mattathias died in 166 B.C., but not before handing the leadership of the rebellion over to his third son, Judas. For the next six years until his own death, Judas won a series of fabulous and unexpected victories. The ultimate underdog, he proceeded to surprise forces far superior to his own, first winning back religious freedom for the Jews, then pressing forward for total independence. His exploits were legendary. He was revered as a folk hero in his own lifetime, though his short life was stained with bloodshed and violence. When he was slain in 160 B.C., his brothers Jonathan and Simon carried on the struggle until Israel's freedom was won in 143 B.C.

I can't emphasize enough the impact that this period was to have on the Jews. Within a decade they had risen from a sluggish, lifeless vassal state within the Greek empire to a proud, uncompromising nation hungry for independence. And the central figure in what was to become their glory days was Judas Maccabeus. He was their great liberator, and his shadow was to be cast long over the subsequent history if Israel. Any future person aspiring to the role of liberator was viewed suspiciously through the template of Judas Maccabeus. He was to cast a long shadow for years to come.

Even though Jonathan and Simon achieved political and religious freedom for Israel, it was lost again in 63 B.C. with the invasion of the next great superpower in ancient history, the Roman Empire. By the time Jesus was an adult, the Jews were anticipating another liberator, one who would do as the Maccabees had done and perform the impossible; drive the oppressors into the sea.

When Jesus came with little interest in an immediate release from the subjugation to Rome, he was understandably disappointing to the Jews. There had been a whole string of revolutionaries seeking to imitate the grand exploits of the Maccabees, only to be snuffed out by the might of the Romans. So it was expected that others would follow. If Jesus was to be taken seriously as a possible claimant to the role of Messiah, he would have to come with both barrels blazing. The fact was that Jesus in no way even closely resembled the revolutionary passion of Judas Maccabeus. And for this reason he may have looked like a bit of a joke. Surely you can see why politically Jesus might not have been considered a serious threat during his public life.

John the Baptist, the quintessential prophet

The second person to cast his shadow over the life and times of Jesus was his cousin, John, still known by his nickname, "the Baptist." While Judas set the precedent for Hebrew political leaders, John confirmed all the old stereotypes for Hebrew prophets. He was, if nothing else, ascetic, austere, and fundamentalist.

As an ascetic, John abstained from alcohol and meat. He lived on locusts and wild honey. The community of his disciples often fasted and prayed for extended periods. They shunned conventional comforts. John himself wore camel's skin and lived a relatively nomadic existence in the wilderness around the River Jordan. I always imagine him to be a hairy, unkempt wild man from the desert. Additionally, he was a stern, often angry preacher, railing against the excesses of both the civil and religious leaders of his time. His calls to repentance and his demands for a righteous, holy lifestyle were reminiscent of the great Hebrew prophets mentioned before. In fact, he was everything we imagine these prophets to have been. He fulfilled the stereotype perfectly.

There has been much discussion about whether John was in some way connected with the Essene community at Qumran. This was the group of fundamentalist ascetics who had left the materialism and the excess of modern Hebrew life in Jerusalem to recreate the Jewish ideal in the hills of the Palestinian wilderness. They fasted regularly. They made exhaustive studies of the Hebrew Bible and had a large library, much of which formed the basis of what we now call the Dead Sea Scrolls. They devoted themselves to a strict discipline, not unlike the great monastic orders of early Christianity. They had a commitment to uphold old-time Judaism. In a sense they saw themselves as the true custodians of the religion of Moses. There is no direct evidence that ties them to John the Baptist, but the similarity between them is unmistakable. John was a stern disciplinarian, a fundamentalist and an ascetic, and it was for these very reasons that he was taken so seriously. When he came into the desert "as a voice crying in the wilderness," he was immediately discernable as a prophet. He looked and acted like one. And not only was his appearance in keeping with his role, but so was his message.

Repent. Return to your roots as Jews. Renew your vows to live righteous, holy lives. It was everything one expected a Hebrew prophet to say. When someone comes looking like a man of God, acting like a prophet and sounding like one too, you had better take notice. You don't want to take any chances.

Inasmuch as he was taken so seriously so quickly, John became dangerous to the civil and religious leaders very early in his career. And *especially* inasmuch as he took it upon himself to demand the fruit of repentance not only from the common people but also from the leadership of Israel, he was soon considered subversive. His condemnation of the Pharisees and the Sadducees, two powerful groups of Jewish religious leaders, is recorded by Matthew as being scathing, even vitriolic. It was clear he wasn't going to last very long in public life. To make matters worse, after calling the religious leaders a pack of vipers, he turned his attention to the civil authorities and condemned Herod for having taken his brother's wife to bed and marrying her. It was the last straw. If he were just some crazy maniac, ranting and raving in the desert, no one would have paid him the least bit of attention. But he was more than that. He was dangerous. And dangerous people are usually dealt with very quickly. Herod threw him in prison and eventually had him executed.

Jesus was taken far less seriously. The religious leaders sent emissaries to try to trick or taunt him. Because he was not considered a threat, there was no drastic action. At first, he was just a nuisance and was treated with contempt and disdain. It was not until well into his public ministry that these leaders considered it necessary for Jesus to be eliminated. As for the civil authorities, throughout Jesus' life they could never see what all the fuss was about. Only at his birth did King Herod consider him worthy of his attention, with tragic consequences. Even at the end of his life, the government officials and rulers who were implicated in Jesus' so-called trial found the whole business a distasteful distraction.

But John was a different matter because he looked much more like the expected stereotype than did Jesus. Bear in mind the Maccabean revolts had occurred only a few generations previously. The Hebrews craved a new religio-political leader more than anything. No wonder they had the temerity to come right out and ask John whether he was the Messiah. John's denial was, no doubt, shocking to them all. And yet in many respects it may have confirmed what they expected because it pointed the way to an even more impressive, even more fearsome leader of God's people.

"After me," he cried, "will come one who is more powerful than I, whose sandals I am not fit to carry. He will baptise you with the Holy Spirit and fire. His winnowing fork is in his hand and he will clear his threshing floor, gathering wheat into the barn and burning up the chaff with unquenchable fire" (Matthew 3:11–12).

To John's listeners, such a description would have been reminiscent of the stories they had heard their grandfathers tell about the great Judas Maccabeus and his fearless brothers. And yet the man who was to fulfill these words was nothing like the Maccabeans. Jesus was fearless and he was a revolutionary. But so revolutionary was he as to be readily misunderstood by those around him. The legacies of the Maccabeans and of John the Baptist were, in fact, to cloud the identity of the Messiah longer than might otherwise have been the case. By comparison, Jesus seemed laughable. And as a result he lasted longer in public ministry than might have been expected.

Jesus the unlikely prophet

Unlike John, Jesus was not an ascetic. He liked to eat and drink and to engage in the garrulous, raucous celebrations that were so much a part of Jewish culture. He was not disdainful of the way common people embraced life with gusto and vigor. He never advocated a rejection of the prevailing culture but rather spoke as a man keenly in touch with such notions as celebration and community. He was likely to be seen as a crude, robust northerner. It was often noted that those from Galilee, a province in the north of Palestine, were far less sophisticated that the southerners from around Jerusalem. In fact, they were treated with some contempt by the southerners.

Many years before, owing to pressure by the non-Jewish nations further to the north, Galilee found itself somewhat cut off from the rest of Jewish Palestine. The Galileans were surrounded by Samaritans, the Phoenicians and the Syrians—all Gentile nations. As a result, when the process of hellenization was at its peak, Galilee became an easy target, almost completely losing its Jewish heritage. During the revolts of Judas Maccabeus, the faithful Jews were actually withdrawn to the south for nearly half a century. This meant that after independence for Israel was won, Galilee had to be recolonized. And this fact, together with its diversity of population, contributed to the contempt felt for Galileans by southern Jews.

In fact, there is a delightful vignette recorded in John's Gospel (1:43–51) in which a young man named Philip, having encountered Jesus very early in his public ministry, finds his friend Nathanael and excitedly tells him of the remarkable man he has just met.

"We have found the very one Moses wrote about in the Law and about whom the prophets wrote," he exclaimed excitedly, no doubt tantalizing Nathanael, who would have responded eagerly by asking him who it was: John the Baptist? Another Maccabean? Someone else?

"Jesus of Nazareth—the son of Joseph," announced Philip. And Nathanael's heart sank.

"Nazareth in *Galilee!*" he scoffed. "Can anything good come out of Nazareth?"

And yet it wasn't just a common grassroots disdain for the northern Galileans that was evident in Jewish life. This disdain had been installed in their written code to some degree. During a discussion among the Pharisees about Jesus there arose the suggestion that perhaps the Nazarene ought to be brought into their midst to defend himself. This was scoffed at by the leaders. "Look into it," they snarled, "and you will find that a prophet does not come out of Galilee" (John 7:52). Of course, what was unbeknown to them at that time was the fact that Jesus had originally been born in the south in the royal city of Bethlehem before moving with his family to Nazareth.

In fact, even Nazarenes found it hard to accept that Jesus was a great prophet. As his reputation as a radical new thinker eventually began to grow throughout Israel, those back home in Nazareth were amazed. "Where did this man get these things?" they marvelled. "What is this wisdom that he has acquired, that he even performs miracles. Isn't this the carpenter? Isn't this Mary's son and the brother of James, Joseph, Judas, and Simon? Aren't his sisters here with us?" (see Mark 6:1–5). Jesus countered their disdain with the truism that a prophet is usually without honor in their hometown.

This episode raises some fairly serious questions for me. Here was Jesus, the Son of God, walking on earth and transforming lives and reframing his culture's perception of life and faith. And yet those who lived with him for the thirty years before he commenced his public ministry never saw anything in him that would indicate he was the promised Messiah. When he finally did embark on that ministry, they were taken by surprise and said, "Where did he get all this stuff? He's just Jesus, our local carpenter!"

What does that tell you? To me, it says that Jesus must have been remarkably down-to-earth—so real, so much like ordinary people—as to not stand out from the crowd. Does that bother you? If your picture of Jesus has him as some other-worldly, cosmic holy man, you would imagine the Nazarenes responding to Jesus' public ministry with something like, "We always knew Jesus was different. He wasn't like most people around here. It doesn't surprise me at all that he has gone public with all this religion."

Shattering expectations

But Jesus just was not what anyone expected. In fact, his first recorded miracle took place in Galilee at, of all places, a wedding feast. A wedding banquet then was not a sophisticated, genteel reception like ours today in which the members of the bridal party sit like mounted exhibits in their morning suits and taffeta gowns at the bridal table. A Galilean wedding was a rough-and-ready affair. It usually went on for eight days and included an orgy of eating and drinking and celebrating.

In those days, a father prepared himself for his daughter's wedding the day she was born. Each year when he was fermenting his family's batch of wine, the father would draw out an extra barrel for his young daughter's wedding day. As girls were usually married off at around the age of sixteen, most fathers would have had sixteen barrels of superbly aged wine stashed away in their cellar. It was the custom to bring out the wine in order of maturity so that the best wine, which had been sitting way back down in the corner of the cellar for sixteen years, was brought out first. The new wine was brought out when everyone was too tipsy to notice.

Now while Jesus and his disciples were enjoying themselves at this, the most raucous and robust of all Jewish feasts, the unimaginable happened. The host ran out of wine (John 2:1–11). It was a truly embarrassing moment. The father of the bride, his daughter and his new son-in-law would have had to live with the humiliating memory that the wine ran out before the eight days of celebration were through. Few things in Hebrew culture would have been so mortifying.

Without alcohol, the recognized lubricant of community celebrations, the party would quickly break up and leave the host family alone with their embarrassment. And remember, most fathers would not have taken their responsibility for their daughter's wedding lightly. In other words, the chances are that this party had been through quite a bit of alcohol by this stage. It would be fair to assume that most of them were three sheets to the wind when the wine ran out.

What did Jesus do? He turned over sixty liters of water into wine. Not just rough red either. The master of ceremonies was amazed that the wine served up by Jesus was of an even superior quality to the wine served on the first day. I've heard a few people turn themselves inside out trying to explain that it was really non-alcoholic cider or unfermented grape juice that he conjured. But there's not one ancient version of John's Gospel that does not make it clear that it was alcohol—and the best quality, too!

I've always thought it was no small matter that Jesus used six stone jars usually filled by the Jews for ceremonial washing in which to conjure the wine. Was this his little joke? The strictly religious Jews considered so many things unclean that they encouraged a regimen of ceremonial cleansings whenever the faithful came into contact with something that was considered unholy. The slightest infraction of the rules, they said, meant the loss of God's favor.

When Jesus performed his first miracle it was the creation of alcohol that he knew would continue to fuel the raucous celebration in the little town of Cana. He did it in ceremonial jars as if to suggest that he had come to give life, not to bind life as the ceremonial system had done. At the risk of reading too much into it, perhaps it is a backhanded shot at the Jewish leaders who used the purification laws to marginalize ordinary people and separate them from God. Jesus' miracle shatters the old system of drawing heavy lines between the holy and the profane, the accepted and the unacceptable. Via Jesus now everyone can be accepted.

The best man at Jesus' banquet

So John was an ascetic and Jesus was not. John was austere and Jesus was not. Or at least, Jesus was rarely so. We often emphasise his sternness and solemnity and these were occasionally traits that we find captured in the Gospels. It is true that he drove the money-lenders out of the Temple and that he was involved in an escalating confrontation with the Pharisees. In fact, he could be quite scathing in his remarks about them (and to them). And, of course, his teaching was occasionally sobering. But Jesus was the whimsical man who took the time to watch the lilies of the field swaying in the breeze (Matthew 6:28), who laughed and played with children (Matthew 11:16), and who was often criticized for enjoying himself too much (Matthew 11:19). He was the enchanting storyteller whose parables were not only works of art but also often humorous and sometimes hilarious.

I've heard it described that the difference between John and Jesus is like that between a dirge and a dance. This is not to imply one is right and the other is wrong. Their ministries and their contributions to the life of Israel fit together like a hand in a glove. John was calling the people back to the fundamentals of their faith, and Jesus was then redefining those fundamentals in liberating and profound new ways.

In this case, the "fundamentalist" and the "liberal" were a perfect relay team. John recognized this himself when he saw that the multitudes that had once flocked to hear his stern message of repentance were now deserting him to listen to Jesus. John's disciples expressed their concern that they were losing their clientele, but the Baptist (a truly wise man) replied, "You yourselves can testify that I said: 'I am not the Messiah, but am sent ahead of him'" (John 3:28).

He saw himself as the best man and Jesus as the groom. In this motif, the people are the bride. The preparation is done by the best man, but the bride belongs to the groom. There is a very real sense in which the move from fundamentalism to radicalism is implied here. To move from chaos to new life almost always involves a process of fundamentalism. John saw himself as only a passing phase pointing to better things. Sadly, many onlookers mistook him for the better things. This is a common mistake. No one prefers chaos, so the step to fundamentalism is often an easy one. But the ensuing step, the breaking away from the restrictive blind allegiance to a rule or discipline to the embracing of a radical, liberating new freedom, is by far a more difficult step. John was quite prepared to make it, but for the fact that his life was cut tragically and unnecessarily short. Unfortunately, many others were far less willing to do so.

Jesus was clearly aware of the degree to which he was being compared with his predecessors, especially John the Baptist. In fact, he could even see the funny side of it. When he was criticized for enjoying life too much and not fasting as much as John, he perhaps laughed and said, "When John the Baptist came neither eating bread nor drinking wine you said, 'He has a demon.' The Son of Man came eating and drinking and you say, 'Here is a glutton and a drunkard, a friend of tax collectors and sinners'" (Luke 7:33–34).

It is as if Jesus was saying: "I can't win. If I came as a wild, vegetarian, teetotaling, desert-dwelling, camel-skin-wearing, Bible-thumping preacher, you'd think me insane. But when I come as a man connected with his culture and to those around him, able to enjoy good food and wine, able to embrace the best aspects of contemporary life, you call me a drunk and a pig."

Jesus the unexpected

So who is to take a glutton and drunkard seriously? Who considers the friend of whores, beggars, thieves, and traitors to be a serious threat to the status quo? Very few people. And there is some evidence to suggest that Jesus was prepared to allow this misconception to occur to some degree. Even when he was at the height of his popularity and was being taken very seriously by those around him as a contender to the role the Maccabeans had played many years before, he seemed prepared to play himself down.

For example, when he finally made it to Jerusalem after a rambling and lengthy tour of Palestine, he was welcomed like a conquering king. Palm leaves were laid before him and the crowds chanted their praises to the "king of Israel" (the church traditionally recalls this event on Palm Sunday, the Sunday before Easter). But how did Jesus enter Jerusalem? Like the new Maccabeus coming to initiate his revolution and drive the Romans into the sea? Far from it. He came into town on a donkey. There is a sense in which Jesus was prepared to accept the misguided adoration of the crowd because he did consider himself worthy of such treatment. After all, he had accepted the ignorant and misguided devotion of the disciples for nearly three years. But his worth, as he saw it, was in his role as the redeeming Messiah, the Son of God, not as the next guerrilla leader struggling for political independence.

I often wonder whether there isn't more than a touch of irony in the way that the man who could play himself down by attending his finest earthly moment on a donkey could also initiate a memorial feast like the Lord's Supper. Can you see the humor in the fact that the man who was accused by his detractors of being a drunkard and a glutton told his disciples to do two things in remembering him when he was gone? What were the two things that this so-called drunkard and glutton asked them to do? To drink and eat!

By all this I don't mean that we ought not to take Jesus seriously. Not at all. What I am suggesting is that Jesus was so unlike the expected and accepted norms regarding religio-political leaders as to almost fool those to whom he came. I don't mean that he was tricking everyone. I mean that he so shattered the standards pushed upon him that the result was quite unexpected. And here lies the great strength of his ministry. It was in being so completely different from the stereotype that he was able to bring new energy to the religious life of Israel at that time.

There had been, and there have been since, countless prophets like John the Baptist (both true and false). And there had been, and there have been since, countless revolutionaries like Judas Maccabeus. Their impact is unquestioned for a period. But their lasting influence becomes lost in the mists of time, to the degree that the teachers of the Law in Israel referred to "the prophets" as one conglomerate. Jesus shattered the mold. His impact has been felt to this very day.

My suggestion is that he did so because he was so radically different, in both style and content, to his predecessors. It was that difference that blinded many of his contemporaries, but the greater payoff was the degree to which it inspired the community that lived with him. So there are grounds, I think, for a reshaping of the pictures we have of Jesus, lest we turn him back into the very stereotype that he smashed.

When predictability is high . . .

I once received a phone call from a woman who had looked my number up in the book under "ministers of religion." Her son had died of a drug overdose. He had been alone in a rented room in a ramshackle beach house on the central coast of New South Wales. She needed a priest to perform the funeral and, since I was the nearest one, she wondered if I would do the job. I said I would be right over. She was a little taken aback. She said she didn't realize we did house calls, but was happy for me to visit.

When I got there, the house was filled with friends and relatives. The dead man had fathered several children to three different women. One of them was interstate, but the other two had gathered with the mourners. A number of big, mean-looking individuals were on the veranda smoking. They wore blue tank tops and were heavily tattooed. I wore what I had on when she called: jeans, sneakers, and a T-shirt. As I approached the house, the mother and two men, who I later discovered were her other sons, called from the front door, "Go away, mate; we've just had a death in the family and we're waitin' for the priest."

"I *am* the priest," I called back.

There was immediate silence and every eye was directed towards me. The curtains in the front room were pulled open and other faces peered at me. I was welcomed in and made very much at home. The group of them opened up to me instantly. We discussed death and dying, the fairness of God, the type of funeral they wanted, the kind of man he had been, his mistakes, his sins and his virtues. All the while I was being offered coffee, tea, beer, cigarettes. Children crawled over me and fought with each other. The mother and girl-friends (who seemed quite friendly with each other) wept openly. Motorbikes came and went, roaring outside as we spoke.

The funeral was rather sad and poorly attended. Everyone felt too ashamed to come into the chapel, I was told. But they were get-ting together for a few drinks after the service. I was invited. I have never conducted a funeral that allowed me so much opportunity for missional engagement. For months after that I was waved to in the street by some of the meanest looking people around. Why? They told me it was because I wasn't like other ministers. I asked them what other ministers were like and they described them as elderly, out of touch, vague, intellectual, arrogant, austere. I then asked them whether they had ever met another minister—I told them I knew a lot of them and they were not often like that at all. No, they answered, they had never really met another minister, come to think of it.

Initially, I was viewed with skepticism, even hostility, because I didn't fit the stereotype. But having broken through that immediate reaction, my differences opened far greater possibilities than if I had conformed to their initial expectations. As I mentioned before, in communication theory when predictability is low, impact is high. This is not that different to what seems to happen with the Gospels with Jesus. He is highly unpredictable, and his impact is unques-tionable. But we need to ask consider what made him so different. And we need to ask whether we have forgotten those differences. I think we are likely to discover another Jesus very different from the one we remember from Sunday school or church. We will discover Jesus the fool.

JESUS THE JESTER

... one is sickened by the chatter of
fussy go-betweens about Christ being
the greatest hero, etc., etc. The humorous interpretation is much better.
—Søren Kierkegaard

What do I mean by saying Jesus was a fool? There are two
levels of meaning. The first is that by this world's standards
of success, prestige, and influence, Jesus can be considered a
failure, a misguided (though commendable) fool. The second level
is the more provocative. It suggests that Jesus actually played the fool
in order to enhance his ministry. I think both are true.

The naiveté of holiness

In his classic work, *In Praise of Folly*, the sixteenth-century hu-
manist Desiderius Erasmus differentiated between the natural fool
and the artificial fool. The natural fool lacks the capacity to reason.
He is a simpleton, naive and innocent. The artificial fool is the
professional clown, the court jester. The artificial fool says, under
the cover of comedy, the things others think, but would never dare
to utter. It was Erasmus' view that Christianity is close to a kind

of natural foolishness; it has a simplicity that suggests its adherents become like little children in order to grasp it.

I know a well-respected churchman with a number of post-graduate degrees in theology and biblical studies who rather proudly says that all he ever preaches is John 3:16 ("For God so loved the world"), so simple is the message of Jesus. Of such so-called natural fools, Alastair Campbell says:

> [They] frequently fail to understand the more complex aspects of human experience, and their lack of ability to predict consequences can at times endanger themselves and others. Yet this lack of sophistication gives a refreshing directness to the simpler person's way of relating to others.[2]

And of course, didn't Jesus, with the ingénue of the young child watching the passing parade, point and shout, "Look, the emperor has no clothes"? The impact of such simplicity lies in its power to expose insincerity and self-deception. In a sense, the fool holds up a mirror in which we can see a reflection of our own hypocrisy. If you read the Gospels, you will see Jesus do this again and again to devastating effect.

Let's face it, on the first level of meaning even the apostle Paul, the great champion of Jesus' cause, recognized the foolishness of the Gospel message of love and grace and forgiveness. He said to the Corinthian church:

> For the message of the cross is foolishness to those who are perishing, but to us who are being saved it is the power of God. . . . God was pleased through the foolishness of what was preached to save those who believe. (1 Corinthians 1:18, 21)

What he is saying is that the simplicity—even the naiveté—of the Gospel is likely to offend the more sophisticated and philosophically astute thinkers of his day. But rather than shirking from the offense of foolishness, Paul embraces it, believing that the very simplicity of Jesus' message was its best feature, not its worst. In fact, he reasoned that it is only when one embraces the folly of the Gospel that one can appreciate its great gravity. In other words, we must become as fools:

> If anyone among you thinks he is wise by this world's standards, he should become a fool, in order to be really wise . . . we are fools for Christ, but you are so wise in Christ. (1 Corinthians 3:18; 4:10)

He is clearly inferring the foolishness of Jesus here. And you can demonstrate Jesus' folly. By the standards of this world he achieved very little. He amassed no personal wealth. He was not widely traveled. He was not highly educated. He left no sons to carry on his name. His short life was spent in the company of common and, in some cases, highly undesirable people. He made dramatic and ambiguous claims regarding his own identity. He was alienated by his own people and then tortured and executed as a young man by the Roman authorities as if he were a criminal. In this regard, Jesus was a fool, and his message of peace and goodwill can appear naive and quite pathetic in the light of his tragic life. Yet his lack of sophistication lent a refreshing directness to Jesus' style of relating to those around him.

The prophetic Jesus

But there's more to it than just Jesus' lack of sophistication. As I said before, there are two levels at which we can say Jesus was a fool. The first is his simple, unworldly approach to life and faith. The second is Jesus' personal prophetic style.

As a prophet, he played the role of the artificial or professional fool with remarkable impact. He was the jester at the court of human arrogance and self interest. And, as we've already noted, it was such a radical change in the people's expectations of a prophet that in his early ministry he was almost unrecognizable in that role.

The classic term "the fool" refers to one who is especially vulnerable to those who hold earthly power and yet who is able to seduce others who are under that same power. He or she does so by reinvesting those people with new meaning and dignity, or alternatively by divesting those powers of their influence. The fool may be easily derided and scoffed at, but he can never be ignored, because he brings a new freshness, a vitality, a new way forward to whatever situation he addresses. It's not unlike the character Touchstone in Shakespeare's *As You Like It*. He is said to use "his folly like a stalking horse and under the presentation of that he shoots his wit." The fool does the same. He stalks, seduces, disarms, and transforms those to whom he comes.

It was also Shakespeare who said, "Fools do often prove prophets," and this is exactly what I have in mind. As the fool, Jesus was able to transform the mindset of his culture and thousands of cultures since by using his foolishness like a stalking horse. The prophet sneaks up on us. Harvey Cox, in a chapter entitled "Christ the Harlequin" from the book *The Feast of Fools,* shares the same insight:

> Like the jester, Christ defies custom and scorns crowned heads. Like a wandering troubadour, he has no place to lay his head. Like the clown in the circus parade, he satirizes existing authority by riding into town replete with regal pageantry when he has no earthly power. Like a minstrel, he frequents dinners and parties. At the end, he is consumed by his enemies in a mocking caricature of royal paraphernalia. He is crucified amidst snickers and taunts with a sign over his head that lampoons his laughable claim.[3]

The role of the jester

The professional jester was a unique and powerful member of the royal court. He was given license to utter the unutterable, to speak the word no court attendant would dare speak. So naturally he accrued great power, being able to influence policy and direct the affairs of the kingdom by highlighting the monarch's folly. It was not a legal power, but it was power nevertheless. When the king became self-absorbed and out of touch with his own convictions in the rarefied atmosphere of the court, it was the fool who invariably was able to reframe his perceptions and find another way of seeing the situation. Of course, the fool managed such a feat by cloaking his message in the warmth of wit and laughter.

There is an old story about a king and his jester that goes like this: Once upon a time there was a king who delighted in his court and all of his subjects. But of all the people in his kingdom, he liked his court jester the best. When he was bothered by the troubles of state, the little court jester could always make him laugh.

One day the king had a great idea. He had the court jester summoned to his chamber. The king was holding a little golden wand and gave it to the jester and said, "My friend, when you find a bigger fool than yourself, you must present to him that little golden wand."

And so the court jester went looking for a bigger fool than himself. He went through every village, asking questions of one and all. Meanwhile, back at the castle his royal highness was taken gravely ill. The jester was called back to be by the king's bedside in his last hours

The dying king said, "Hello, my little friend. I am going on a long journey from which I will never return."

"Your highness," the jester said naively, "have you prepared for this journey?"

"No," replied the dying king, "I haven't."

"Then," laughed the jester, "I must present to you this little golden wand."

The story is told as a reminder that we are foolish if we haven't prepared for our death and for the possibility of another world once we've shuffled off this mortal coil. But it is also a telling illustration of the role of the jester. It radically demonstrates the arrogance, the self-interest, the folly of the monarch. Of course, we always think of jesters wearing funny hats with bells on the end and performing tricks like juggling and joke-telling, like the character in the

"Wizard of Id" comic strip. But I don't necessarily mean that Jesus was a comedian (though some of his parables were intended to get a laugh—as we'll see later). Jesus was a fool in the more prophetic sense of the role.

Donald Capps says: "Folly is a potent form of prophecy because it allows us to see ourselves in a clearer light and prevents us from giving fallible human institutions the honour they are not due." This type of foolishness is at the heart of a lot of Jesus' teaching and is summed up most obviously in his Sermon on the Mount and in his parables. We will take a look at that teaching later. Of course, the role of the fool is not automatically prophetic. Satire can often be heartless and destructive, used as a weapon to protect the perpetrator against any genuine involvement with others. But in the hands of Jesus, the role of the fool takes on remarkable prophetic dimensions.

Nathan the court jester

Another example of this role of court prophet/jester is the Old Testament character called Nathan. He wasn't anywhere near as eccentric as the other Hebrew prophets I mentioned earlier. But he was classic court jester. As a court attendant during the Hebrew monarchy under King David, he was perfectly poised to reframe the perceptions of a king who was growing progressively out of touch with his convictions.

David has been an engaging, charismatic ruler, at one with the people and in touch with the common man. As king, he had a hands-on approach to the affairs of state and led by example. But things began to change. He became increasingly disinterested in his regal duties: "In the spring, at the time when kings go off to war, David sent Joab out with the king's army. . . . But David remained in Jerusalem."[4]

Bored with life at court, during the army's absence David engaged in his infamous dalliance with Bathsheba, the wife of one of his soldiers (this was certainly taking his hands-on approach too far!). Actually, it was a shameful abuse of his regal privilege to have her brought to his bed like some home-delivered pizza. Furthermore, David tried to use his influence as king to trick her husband, Uriah, into believing the resulting pregnancy was his own doing. When his intrigues failed because of Uriah's scrupulous integrity, David again abused his position by having Uriah placed in the front line of battle and thus killed by the Ammonites. Lost in self-deception and drunk on his seemingly limitless power, David had descended into near madness. This section of the saga ends ominously:

> When Uriah's wife heard that her husband was dead, she mourned for him. After the time of mourning was over, David had her brought to his house, and she became his wife and bore him a son. But the thing David had done displeased the Lord. (2 Samuel 11:26–27)

In other words, for all intents and purposes, he had got away with it. No member of the court would have dared accuse their monarch of unbridled lust, rape, sexual harassment, deceit, murder—all of which are demonstrated in the passage. But God was displeased with him (surely one of the classic understatements of the Bible) and his man, Nathan the prophet, was to give voice to God's unhappiness. It was left to the fool to speak the words no one else would dare utter. And only as a fool could he get a hearing from the increasingly despotic king.

Nathan entered the scene and offered his monarch a story. Perhaps David expected some frivolous entertainment, or an allegory to stretch his mind. What he received was a smack in the teeth. But my point is this: Nathan could only say what he did under the cover of folly. He was just like Touchstone. In Nathan's court tale there are two men: one very wealthy, the other very poor.[5] The wealthy man has abundant sheep and cattle. The poor man has just one sheep, which he raised by hand from infancy. He looks upon the animal as even more than a pet, as his own child. When a traveler arrives at the home of the wealthy man, he takes the poor man's only sheep and slaughters it to feed the guest.

Nathan then paused, as if to say, "Well, your majesty, what do you think about that?" and in so doing he invited David to condemn one who would commit so callous an act of selfishness. Typically, David, who was known for wearing his heart on his sleeve, ranted and raved and screamed his outrage. The wealthy man ought to be severely dealt with, he argued. And then the fool, the naive, simple fool delivered the *coup de grace*: "You are that man!"

These four words immediately reframed David's understanding of his own actions. Once seduced by his own power, the self-deceived king now saw the abhorrent behavior that up until that point he may well have tried to justify. This was the fool as a prophet. The sensible powerful members of the court might have tried to broach with David his own disgraceful activity, but the fool told him a whimsical tear-jerker about another evil man—and in doing so transformed the situation and the resulting behavior. David immediately saw his actions for what they were and entered a painful period of repentance and restitution.

Nathan's potent use of the parable was to be imitated to far greater effect many, many years later by a descendent of the same King David. Jesus' parables are devastating examples of his role as a prophet/jester. In a very real sense, just as Nathan was God's anointed mouthpiece in the court of the Davidic monarchy, so is Jesus the jester in the court of human affairs generally. To the arrogance, pride, and self-deception of all men and women, Jesus the fool has a profoundly important word to speak.

Jonah the reluctant fool

Sometimes it is not the teller of a biblical story who acts like a professional fool to make his point. Sometimes it is a character in a story who has the same profound effect on the listeners. The story about Jonah is a classic of this kind. We don't know who wrote this biting little tract, but we think it was constructed during or after the fifth century B.C., just after the Jews had returned from a long and bitter exile as slaves to the Babylonians. Many of the returnees had begun to develop a very defensive and parochial response to the non-Jewish world. Some of their leaders were forbidding Jews to marry women outside their faith, and those who already had married were being urged to divorce the poor women and discard them to a life of prostitution or begging. It was a difficult time for Israel.

We all know what it is like to have been betrayed or hurt by someone else (some, of course, know it far better than others). Our response, often, is to withdraw and withhold our trust from others, even those who deserve it. It is a natural defensive action. Like a snail withdraws into its shell, so do we retreat from further human contact after a painful experience in relationship. Often the clearest, most tragic example of this is the example of a rape victim. One retreats from any meaningful contact or physical touch after this, the ultimate betrayal. Well, in many respects Israel had been raped and was, at this point in its history, refusing to trust anyone. The Israelites' response may not have been wise, but it was certainly understandable.

It was in the midst of this kerfuffle that some unknown subversive storyteller told the story of one of Israel's ultimate fools. His name was Jonah, and the story that bears his name is one of the funniest yet strangest in the Bible. The author seems to be countering the parochial ideas of Israel's leadership by presenting God's views towards Gentiles in comic contrast. The story opens with: "Now the word of the Lord came to Jonah the son of Amittai, saying, 'Arise, go to Nineveh, that great city, and cry against it; for their wickedness has come up before me.'"[6]

Now there have been times when I have been preaching in my church and have made a comment or used an illustration that cuts very near to the bone among my congregation. One of the very interesting responses to such an incident is that some of my listeners will laugh. It is a tight, nervous laugh. Because what I have said is so confronting or painful some have found themselves (almost involuntarily, I suggest) laughing with anxiety. It is a spooky phenomenon.

I think that many Jews in the fifth century B.C. would have been struck by the parallels between their situation, having just come out of a terrible exile, and the situation of the people during the time of Jonah. The story of Jonah is set during the eighth century, during which the Assyrian Empire was exiling the Israelites and oppressing them in much the same way as the Babylonians were to do three centuries later. Here God is telling a prophet to go and save the Assyrian Ninevites. In other words, God is telling Jonah to rescue people just like the oppressive, merciless Babylonians that the hearers of the story would have just escaped. I can almost hear their nervous laughter. In all history, no Hebrew prophet had ever been sent to the Gentiles, let alone to the worst enemy from among the Gentiles, the people from the nation that had exiled them from their beloved land.

Next the clever author of this story has the main character, the prophet Jonah, pantomime Israel's response to such a word from the Lord. Jonah operates in much the same way that those who first hear the story might have reacted. I'm sure you remember how it goes: "But Jonah arose to flee Tarshish, from the presence of the Lord. He went down to Joppa and found a ship going to Tarshish; he paid the fare and went on board, to go with them to Tarshish, away from the presence of the Lord."[7]

Just as his readers couldn't bear the thought of bringing a word of salvation to their former oppressors, neither could Jonah. He determined to flee to the end of the known world, as Tarshish (Spain) was then considered, in order to dodge God's surveillance. Well, one tragicomical situation after another befell him, each one funnier than the last, until the climax in which Jonah was swallowed by a fish. Jonah was now the fool, the laughable idiot, around whom the most preposterous of tragedies take place. The audience is invited to laugh at someone who thinks he can escape from God. But this is still nervous laughter because all the time there lies the nagging concern that they may very well be laughing at themselves.

Jonah was a narrow and parochial man who thought God was only God on Hebrew soil. Remember this was the prevailing mood in Israel at that time, so that by laughing at the foolishness of Jonah and his theological system, his readers were forced to mock themselves and their own religious leaders. The idea of God following Jonah to the ends of the earth and encountering him in the belly of a fish would have struck at the very heart of the people's worldview. And, of course, it was all couched in such ridiculously funny terms. That was the spoonful of sugar that helped the medicine go down.

Not only this, but when Jonah, after his conversion and restoration, returned to Nineveh to do the dirty deed and preach a prophetic message of forgiveness, something terrible happened! The Assyrians repented and believed, and God spared them. If it isn't bad enough that the prophet had to preach forgiveness to them, it was even worse when they were all actually forgiven. God stayed his hand of judgment. They were all saved.

But Jonah was furious. He had been made a fool of because his word of destruction was not fulfilled. The magic and comical details of the story continued as God made a tree grow to give shade to Jonah as he sulked outside the city walls. Then God caused it to wither and die. This petty event was the last straw for poor old Jonah. He pitched a fit. The scene was genuinely funny until the storyteller had God's voice thunder into the picture:

> You pity the plant [says God], for which you did not labor, nor did you make it grow, which came into being in a night and perished in a night. And should I not pity Nineveh, that great city, in which there are more than a hundred and twenty thousand people who do not know their right hand from their left, and so many cattle? (Jonah 4:10–11)

How about this great concern for the cattle! Anyway, Jonah was a fool, there is no doubt. He was a fool because he believed he could escape the presence of a universal God and he was a fool because he dared to consider it a disappointment when 120,000 pagans were spared by God's grace. His foolishness is couched in ridiculous terms, littered with unlikely and comical scenes, all of which combine to reframe the readers' perceptions. By laughing at Jonah, you have to side with God. And when you side with this God, you side with a God whose presence and whose grace are universal. In the parochial, exclusivist culture of Israel in the fifth century before Christ, Jonah the fool radically reframes the issue.

The feast of fools

Of course, it's not only in the Bible that we can find examples of this foolish kind of prophecy. Alastair Campbell tells the story of Narrenfest, the medieval Feast of Fools, wherein the authority of the church is attacked by the potent use of folly:

> Narrenfest, the Feast of Fools, was a kind of anti-Mass celebrated by the younger clergy in defiance of the bishop and his established orders. Beginning on the first of January (the Day of Circumcision), it continued until Epiphany. The "celebrants" wore masks and fantastic costumes, banqueted at the altar, celebrated an obscene parody of the ritual of Mass and even, on occasion, worshiped an ass as the "Lord of Disorder."[8]

As you can guess, the official line of the church was to condemn roundly this kind of outrageous behavior. But as best we can tell, it was practiced from the twelfth to the fifteenth century—maybe even as late as the seventeenth century. Its purpose, no doubt, was to let off a little steam in the context of a stultifying, oppressive church structure but, more than that, it mocked the undue importance attributed to that structure.

Elements of Narrenfest were harsh and cutting. In our modern context, a similar role is played by our regular newspaper cartoonists, who by the sting of their wit are able to display the foibles or excesses of our political leaders. In some cases, the cartoonist can be horribly cruel in caricaturing not only the actions of public figures but their physical appearance as well. Such is often the case with satire. It can be heartless and destructive. I am not wanting to suggest that Jesus was merely a clever satirist or that he ever descended to cruelty. However, he was able to mock and undermine the overbearing establishment of his day in powerful ways.

Professional fools throughout history have often been nothing more than mere satirists. And, at worst, they have been cruel and unfair to the "freaks" of their societies—the mentally retarded, the physically disabled, the emotionally damaged.

I have a sister who is intellectually disabled. She works in a factory as a process worker. She lives in a hostel that cares for developmentally disabled adults. She has a very full and happy life (sometimes more happy than mine, I think). But I can recall as a child that I couldn't stand Jerry Lewis movies on TV because I felt that his grotesque clowning looked too much like poking fun at people like my sister. While I'm sure that wasn't intended, his kind of foolery felt too cruel for my liking. And many clowns, both modern and ancient, have used such people as models for their bizarre performances.

Jesus was not at all like this. In fact he, like no other, embraced the marginalized and oppressed members of his community and filled them with a sense of dignity and self-respect. But in many ways he was something of a clown. I felt the musical *Godspell* helped open our minds to the possibility of Jesus and his disciples being seen as a traveling band of troubadours, spreading gaiety and humor around in the lives of an oppressed people. And remember this guise of a clown is not all smiles and laughter. The clown is at once both tragic and comic. And surely Jesus is both of these things.

But just as Jesus is no mere satirist, neither is he merely a clown. The well-known incident where he drove the corrupt money-changers from the temple in Jerusalem in Matthew 21:12 indicates a man of considerable inner strength and fortitude, a man of resolve, a serious and thoughtful man of faith. So does the occasion in Matthew 23:27–28, where he bellowed into the faces of the religious leaders of his day that they were like white-washed tombs, all shiny and clean on the outside and full of rotting corpses within.

In fact, this episode occurs in a section in Matthew's Gospel that is often referred to as the Seven Woes, a catalogue of the sins of the Pharisees and the teachers of the Law. No stupid clown could have tabulated this chronicle of insights. We do Jesus a great disservice not to take him seriously. This was a mistake of many of his religious contemporaries, as we have already noted.

So he is not simply a satirist. Nor is he some blithe nincompoop. Yet he is a fool. And a rousing one at that. The American College Dictionary defines that term as:

> fool (fool), n. 1. one who lacks sense; a silly or stupid person. 2. a professional jester, formerly kept by a person of rank for entertainment . . .

Here we have Erasmus' natural fool and artificial fool. Jesus is delightfully both at the same time. As the natural fool, his simplicity and naiveté are refreshing and confronting. Jesus is very much like the title character in Dostoyevsky's *The Idiot*, in which Prince Myshkin appears dim-witted and socially inept, his open simplicity leading people to regard him as a fool because he does not conform to the insincerities and cynical self-seeking of the society to which he belonged. As non-conforming outsiders both Myshkin and Jesus notice things other people never notice. Such a simple honesty is both fascinating and infuriating.

This quality has best been captured on film in the Peter Sellers movie, *Being There*. Sellers plays a socially retarded gardener called Chance. He has spent every moment of his life behind the imposing walls of a grand old Edwardian mansion in America, tending the elaborate garden of the owner. When she suddenly dies, he is cast out into the real world. All he has ever known has been her garden. He has never watched television, read a newspaper, been to a restaurant, touched the ocean, seen a skyscraper. He is so alienated as to appear like a little child.

And yet he falls in with the beautiful and influential people of Washington and becomes known as Chauncy Gardener. Whenever asked for his opinion, he answers with allusions to gardening and plant life. Those cynical leaders who encounter him in the corridors of power find a refreshing and powerful wisdom in his quaint illustrations. By the end of the film, Chauncy is being touted as a possible presidential candidate. He is considered a financial wizard and a political genius. Another film that attempts (with mixed success) to capture the ingénue of Jesus' personal style is the French/Canadian director Denys Arcand's *Jesus of Montreal*. But Jesus is more than Prince Myshkin, Chauncy Gardener, or Arcand's character, Daniel. He is also the professional jester, parrying and thrusting against the conventional wisdom of his (and our) day. There is a very clear sense in the Gospels that Jesus was not just some idiot led about by the nose by those in religious or political power. He was the subversive critic of those powers, able to be so under the cover of his simplicity and naiveté.

Have you ever started work at a new job and found yourself using your ignorance about the workings of the new place to your advantage? We all have. There have been times when we can use our inexperience to great effect. Even when we know something is probably not being done correctly, we're happy to smile wide-eyed and say "Gee, I didn't realize that's the way it's normally done." Actually, I have achieved a great deal sometimes under the guise of being uninformed about a new situation. I don't want to suggest that Jesus was being quite so cunning, but I do think that he was prepared to take full advantage of his disarming simplicity and honesty.

Like the jester in the court of human affairs, Jesus refuses to allow us to become self-absorbed and out of touch with reality. He condemns us when we become drunk with our own power and infatuated with our position of influence. He repeatedly reminds us of our failings and our shortcomings. He holds our hypocrisy up to us like a mirror before a vain person. Time and again he cuts incisively and deeply to the heart of our frailties and demands we take into account our abuses and excesses. And yet he does so in the most odd, whimsical, comical ways.

Most importantly, Jesus does this without interest in personal gain. And here is the striking thing about his foolishness: there is nothing in it for him. The jester might have been rewarded on a per-laugh basis—the more laughs you get, the more money you make. But not Jesus. His interest is only in truth and justice. For me personally, this is the most shocking aspect of Jesus' ministry. There really is nothing in it for him. He reframes our perceptions about ourselves, our faith, our sin, our guilt, our religion, simply for our own benefit.

Jesus' way of relating to people

There are two ways of relating to people. One way is to see them as objects, to see them for what function they serve for us. The best example I can think of is the way we view automatic teller machines at the bank. We see them for their function (giving us our money) and we have no regard for how the ATM feels about the transaction. It is an object with the function of serving us. When we treat people this way, we do a great deal of damage to them. Have you ever stood in a line at McDonalds and become frustrated when the other lines move more quickly than yours? The quiet rage you feel within at the slowness of the girl serving your line is the same detached frustration we usually reserve for machines. Now we feel that irritation towards a living human being. It's as if we see her as having no value other than to fulfill her function to serve us. Martin Buber, a German theologian, wrote about this phenomenon and said that when we treat people as objects we see them as "it."

The other way to see people is as subjects, letting ourselves be aware that they have feelings about what is happening even as we do. Buber says this is treating people as "thou." He believes we have become too accustomed to using people (as "it") rather than loving them (as "thou"). His I–Thou theology, though hard to understand, hits the nail right on the head. He says God relates to each of us in an I–Thou kind of way. He never uses us to meet his needs. He is always aware of how we feel and what we need. On the other hand, our relationship to God, if we do it right, will also be I–Thou.

False religion tries to suggest that we can use God, to push the right heavenly buttons so that he will come good with whatever we want or need. In other words, we can bribe him with pious actions or flattering words. But that type of religion only makes God an object, someone we can use. True religion, says Martin Buber, teaches us to meet God, not to manipulate him.

Likewise, Jesus' interest is to meet us, not make use of us for his own benefit. There is nothing in it for him other than the basic satisfaction of having secured for people he loves ("thou") a more enriched, more fulfilled way of living. This is truly foolishness in a world grown used to manipulation, coercion, and subjugation. In fact, it may be here that Jesus proves beyond any doubt what a fool he can be. That the most perceptive, dynamic, intuitive mind this world has ever seen allowed himself to be humiliated, vilified, misunderstood, and ultimately destroyed is proof positive of his folly.

As charming and as winsome as he may have appeared, there was a great clarity of thought evident in Jesus. He had a devastating wit and a superior intelligence, paradoxically cloaked in a simplicity that proved most disarming. He was able to attack subtly racial prejudice by creating a hero out of a hated Samaritan. He lifted the place of women by often making them examples of faith. He demonstrated foolhardy courage and daring abandon in his criticism of the structures of authority around him. He was a strange and wonderful man who taught us how to see the world with different eyes. We need new eyeglasses with which to see our world. I believe Jesus became that new vision for us. He showed us another way to see the same old things.

A fresh look at Jesus

We also seem to need new glasses with which to see Jesus. We tend to have forgotten him as a thinker or theologian. We have become conditioned to think only of Paul, Luke, John, and Peter and the rest of the New Testament authors as theological thinkers. Jesus is seen as the agent of God's grace and as the great redeemer who ushers in the kingdom but as one whose teaching was more concerned with ethical matters than theological content.

Paul is often seen as the great Christian theologian and, as a result, most preachers make extensive use of his material. I often say that the Gospel accounts of Jesus are the best kept secrets in Christianity. I think some of the reason for this imbalance in our use of the New Testament has to do with the agenda we bring to our reading of the Bible.

I've heard it said that in the southern US churches during the civil rights movement, this was glaringly apparent. On one tragic Sunday, in Birmingham, Alabama, someone threw a Molotov cocktail into the Sunday school of a black church. It was a senseless act of violence against innocent children and it sparked an outcry from both sides of the debate. One newspaper thought to survey all the churches of the city to find out what their preachers were using as the text for their sermon that particular morning. Without fail, all the white pastors were preaching from Paul and the black pastors were preaching from one or other of the Gospels. In other words, the white churches were dealing with heavy, philosophical/theological considerations. The black churches were looking at the details of Jesus' life and thought. Their agendas determined what parts of the Bible they looked at.

My contention is that we are mistaken if we assume we will find only philosophical theology in Paul and only ethics in Jesus. That is a disservice to both. In the Gospels you find a man who can reframe the way our tired, cynical, self-righteous world has come to view life. If you are burnt out and feeling that the only thing you have less of than money is spiritual conviction, Jesus the fool can provide the very reframe you are looking for.

THE ART OF REFRAMING

I have used the term "reframe" several times already and not yet fully explained what I mean by it. In order to understand what Jesus was doing, I think it is important that we know what it is to "reframe" a situation or a mindset. Jesus was reframing again and again in the Gospels. In fact, I believe it is one of the chief tools he employed in his teaching style. In order to see Jesus the fool in action, you need to understand how (and why) he reframed the circumstances or the thinking of those with whom he dealt.

Reframing

Reframing is simply changing the frame in which someone perceives events in order to change their meaning. When the meaning changes, the person's responses and behaviors also change. It is a technique used in counseling by the school of therapists who practice neuro-linguistic programming (NLP). These therapists realize that the meaning of any event depends on the frame in which it is perceived. By changing the frame, and thereby the meaning, the counselor can assist the client in moving forward from situations that had once held them back.

While there is more to NLP than just the technique of reframing, two NLP books that really highlighted the impact of changing frames for clients in counseling situations were *Frogs Into Princes* and *Reframing*, both by Richard Bandler and John Grinder. They aren't the easiest books to read since they are mostly transcripts of workshops in reframing techniques, but I find them fascinating nonetheless.

They illustrate what reframing is with an old Chinese Taoist story about a farmer in a poor country village:

> He was considered very well-to-do, because he owned a horse which he used for plowing and for transportation. One day his horse ran away. All his neighbors exclaimed how terrible this was, but the farmer simply said, "Maybe."

> A few days later the horse returned and brought two wild horses with it. The neighbors all rejoiced at his good fortune, but the farmer just said, "Maybe."

> The next day the farmer's son tried to ride one of the wild horses; the horse threw him and broke his leg. The neighbors all offered their sympathy for his misfortune, but the farmer again said, "Maybe."

> The next week conscription officers came to the village to take young men for the army. They rejected the farmer's son because of his broken leg. When the neighbors told him how lucky he was, the farmer replied, "Maybe."[9]

See how the meaning of any event can be altered given a different frame? Having two wild horses is a good thing until it is seen in the context of a broken leg. The broken leg seems bad in the context of peaceful village life, but it suddenly becomes good in the context of conscription and war.

We use reframing every time we tell a joke. Most of the situation comedies we watch on TV are based on a reframe (or on the need for a reframe). Reframing is not a new discovery by any means, and Bandler and Grinder are quite prepared to admit it. As I have already noted, it was very clearly part of Jesus' style. But even before Jesus, remember Nathan's parable to King David? In the context of the power-drenched court of an ancient Middle Eastern kingdom, the bringing of a concubine to the bed of a ruler might be an acceptable thing. But in the context of that woman's devoted husband and his love for her alone, it becomes a despicable act of selfishness. Nathan's story provides the very reframe that helped David see the real impact of his actions.

Nearly all of Shakespeare's tragedies are based on the misguided perceptions of their main characters. They begin with a situation that needs a reframe, then allow you to watch the tragic repercussions when that reframe is not drawn. The essence of Shakespearean tragedy is to draw from its audience a response of unbearable frustration. Who can sit through *Romeo and Juliet* and not become frustrated at being unable to explain the misapprehensions of the Montagues and the Capulets and thereby save the lovers? When studying *Othello* I couldn't understand why someone didn't just sort out this stupid mess. When watching a performance of the play, I wanted to take the Moor aside and explain in a very civil and orderly fashion that his wife Desdemona was not being unfaithful to him and that Iago was not his closest friend at all, but a slimy, dirty-minded guttersnipe. I wanted to reframe for him.

But this is the key to such tragedy. The Bard wanted us to feel that way. The way it works is to set a scenario wherein the lead character needs to have another (more objective) frame drawn around the events surrounding him. The fact that we can't jump on stage and sort out his misunderstandings and are forced to watch him descend into misery, usually taking several other characters with him, is the dynamic that makes Shakespearean tragedy what it is

Many fables and fairy tales note what it looks like when the frame around certain events or persons is changed. Being a strange looking duckling is hard to take when all your peers poke fun at you for not looking like them. But when seen in the context of that ugly duckling turning into a sleek, beautiful white swan, it becomes a good thing.

My children used to have a delightful book called *Arnold, the Prickly Teddy*, by Kym Lardner. It is about a prickly unloved teddy bear who sits neglected and unwanted in a toy store before being flung onto a rubbish pile. A young boy finds him and takes him home. He has never had a teddy bear before, so he is happy to keep him, no matter how scratchy he feels. Arnold gets carried around everywhere. He goes in the bath with his new friend. He plays with his new friend in the rain, the hail or the sunshine. They sleep together every night. And an interesting thing begins to happen. Slowly the prickles start to wear off and Arnold becomes as smooth and cuddly as all the other popular teddies in the shop. A reframe occurs as you read it. Is it better to start life in the toy shop all soft and cuddly? Or is it better to become soft and cuddly because of love and attention? The one you once felt so sorry for becomes someone to be envied, someone who has grown smooth because life has rubbed up against him.

In general communication theory, it is well known that a signal only has meaning in terms of its context (or frame). Jesus was masterly at offering the signals needed to reframe the thinking of those he encountered. He was not content with anything less than significant change. He orchestrated such change in the minds, hearts, and bodies of individuals by enabling them to think about things differently, the see the world in a new way and to experience new openness. And true to form, he employed the least likely, most surprising techniques to do so. He was truly a fool in the classic sense of the word, using his foolishness to reframe the "wisdom" of his culture and show a new way forward.

The practitioners of NLP are simply making use of a device which is ages old. They have taken into the counseling room a technique that Jesus used on the roadside as he traveled through Palestine. And it works.

Virginia Satir, a leading proponent of NLP, was working with a family in which there was some considerable tension between the father and his adult daughter. He repeatedly accused her of being stubborn. On one occasion, Satir asked the father about his career and found out he was the president of the local bank. He had worked his way up the banking ladder to become a leader in his field. Satir pointed out that this must have taken quite a bit of tenacity on his part. She pressed him to agree that he had had to make some tough decisions and stick to his guns for the good of his business. She then said to him:

> Now I want you to look at your daughter, and to realize beyond a doubt that you've taught her to be stubborn and how to stand up for herself, and that that is something priceless. This gift you've given to her is something that can't be bought, and it's something that may save her life. Imagine how invaluable that will be when your daughter goes out on a date with a man who has bad intentions.[10]

Notice how Virginia Satir has not changed the content of the behavior. Stubbornness is still stubbornness. But she has changed the context in which stubborn behavior can be viewed. Let's face it, there are situations where an unyielding attitude is a great asset. Jesus, in several of his parables, is able to retain the meaning of an event or idea while dramatically changing the context in which it is seen. As we'll see later, the Good Samaritan is a classic example of tenacity being a good thing.

Reframing meaning

I don't mean to suggest that behavior ought not be changed. After all, I don't want to give the impression that every experience in the world and every behavior is appropriate, given some context, some frame. And it's here that I need to differentiate between two types of reframing. The first is "context reframing" where, as we've seen, context shifts—allowing events or action or belief to be see in a new light. The second is called "meaning reframing," where meaning shifts while context remains the same—allowing events or action or belief to change.

What does meaning reframing look like? I heard the story of a counselor who was working with a woman who was a compulsive cleaner. She was so excessive that her family had to make lots of exceptions in order to even live with her. However, her attitude to footprints in the carpet was impossible for them to deal with. Whenever she saw the imprints left by those walking on the pile of the carpet, she was driven to re-vacuum the area where they had stepped.

Can you imagine arriving home from work and having to leap from the front door onto the nearest lounge chair, from there to the next and then make your way through the house as if crossing a stream on top of river stones? The compulsive woman was aware that it was destroying her family, so she went for counseling. The counselor asked her to close her eyes and imagine her carpet without a single footprint on it anywhere. This was bliss for her. She was probably smiling away at this imaginary sight. "And now I want you to realize," the therapist said, "that this means you are totally alone, and the people that you care for and love are nowhere to be seen." Of course, the woman was distressed. The counselor then told her to imagine a few footprints in the carpet and to realize that her loved ones were now around her again. The impact of the exercise was apparently liberating.

This is meaning reframing: the meaning of her cleanliness fetish changed—it isolated her from her family. The content—footprints on the carpet—remained the same, but the meaning attributed to these footprints changed. They could either mean untidiness or they could mean a home full of people. When they were given the latter meaning, the woman felt positive rather than negative about them.

Does this sound manipulative? Didn't each of the counselors in the two cases we have looked at just "trick" the client into seeing things differently? I don't think so. Of course, this technique is open to abuse, as is just about any helping-skills technique. But this is a ministry without guile. The one who naively suggests that maybe a footprinted carpet may mean something other than uncleanliness must do so simply and honestly. This person admittedly holds considerable power and is seeking a manipulation of the other's perception, but is never manipulative in the negative sense.

Those who reframe are seeking to break impasses, making positive change possible. Donald Capps, who has also written on reframing, says that good reframers are not "con-artists" who view others as potential victims; they are "pro-artists" whose creative imagination is for the sole purpose of enabling others to have fuller, more abundant lives.

Reframing by polarity

In many cases, Jesus employs the story/parable form in order to elicit what is today called a polarity response. A polarity response is the exaggerating of a particular position to swing the person sharply back in another direction. Let me illustrate. Suppose I am talking with someone in your church who is really depressed. She is so depressed that I am having trouble making contact with any part of the person that is not down. I can try saying, "You are depressed! You are one of the most depressed people I've ever met. I'll guarantee you've been depressed all your life. You've probably never had any experience other than being down like this, never at all."

"Well, not my whole life, but for the past . . ." they begin.

"Oh no," I press, "I'll bet it's been your whole life."

"No, not my whole life. Last week I was pretty good when my family took me out to dinner for a surprise . . ."

By exaggerating their position, you can get a polarity response. Several of Jesus' stories have exactly the same impact. They get into the mindset or the belief systems of their listeners and they force them to see the result of those systems being pushed to their ultimate (and unsatisfactory) conclusions. By doing this, Jesus forces a response to the other pole, the position he wants to commend to them. In a delightful way, Jesus always seems to do so artlessly and in wide-eyed amazement. It's as if he is saying, "Oh, I see what you mean. Now excuse me while I just push that to its logical conclusion." In every case he makes a mockery of his listeners' prejudice or self-righteousness or arrogance or greed.

A variation on the polarity response technique is psychologist Milton Erickson's advice to clients who want to lose weight. Typically he demands that they gain exactly eleven pounds in the next two weeks. As crazy as it sounds, it actually works very effectively because one of two things happen. Either the person will lose weight—a polarity response—which is the outcome he is working towards anyway, or they will gain eleven pounds. They don't gain ten or twelve pounds. They gain eleven. Erickson says that since they were able to accomplish that, the behavioral presupposition is that they can control their weight! See the clever reframe there? Only a fool asks a person who wants to lose weight to gain weight. That's pretty shrewd "foolishness"!

Jesus made use of this technique time and again. As we'll see in the next chapter, when asked what to do to be saved, he responded by prescribing allegiance to the Law of Moses, the very law most people mistakenly thought he had come to shatter. And by doing so, he elicited a dramatic polarity response.

Reframing by straight prescription

Yet another variation on this reframing technique is "prescription." This involves giving a person a prescription, like a medical doctor prescribing treatment. Erickson, for example, prescribes his client gain eleven pounds. In counseling that prescription may be based on the client's problem, but not necessarily so. The prescription might be a placebo, effective because the client has confidence in it. When prescribing a weight gain, Erickson is after a polarity response. But you can make straight prescriptions when seeking to help people.

Asked to treat a woman who had made multiple suicide attempts, Erickson once prescribed that she foster her love for growing African violets and then give one to every bride married in her local church (where she was a regular member) and to every couple in the congregation to whom a child was born. Twenty years later, he clipped from the local paper an article headed, "African Violet Queen Dies, Aged 76." The prescription was not based on his diagnosis of her problem, but on her confidence in him. He used that confidence to set her reason for living in a new frame.

Jesus made some straight prescriptions. On one occasion, he prescribed a wealthy man to sell everything he had and give it to the poor. A powerful reframe was drawn. And so an effective and inspired prescription can totally reframe a situation. In John 5:2–18 there is a story of quite ridiculous tomfoolery recorded. It concerns a poor lame man who had been lying near the pool at Bethesda for some years. Local lore had it that when the water in the pool began to bubble like a spa bath, the first sick person in the pool would be healed. A man who had put all his hope on being the first into the pool when it bubbled could not find anyone to stay with him twenty-four hours a day on the off chance that the water might rise up. And so he would try to wriggle himself into the pool. Not surprisingly, someone always beat him to it. Can you picture this scene? It would look something like a Monty Python sketch!

So pathetic was he that he had been lying by the pool for thirty-eight years! Jesus came by and asked if he wanted to be healed, then he prescribed a simple response: "Rise, take up your bed, and walk." Immediately, he stood. Jesus reframed the circumstances of this man. It was almost as if this was just too simple to work. He had clung for nearly four decades to a much more elaborate plan.

Another case of straight prescription that reframed matters was employed by Milton Erickson when he was dealing with a couple of restaurateurs, a husband and wife, who were struggling to keep their marriage together. She wanted him to take more control of their affairs, but he believed she ran the restaurant with an iron fist. Erickson discovered that she opened and closed the restaurant every day while he parked or fetched the car. So he made what seemed like a barely consequential prescription: the husband was to go to the restaurant half-an-hour before the wife. So miniscule a change in their routine did this seem that they agreed.

But the simplistic suggestion made a volume of difference. Now he arrived first. He opened up, he owned the keys. She was put completely out of sync. It created such a change in their daily regimen that the terms of their relationship shifted significantly also. By a minimal change in their behavior, he achieved a decisive change in their lives. Rise, pick up your bed and walk! The solutions seem so simple when they are prescribed, but they are never apparent to the people in their midst of their circumstances. They need reframing.

Now again I can hear the more religiously sophisticated of you asking, "Is he suggesting that Jesus' miracles of healing were only psychologically based?" That's a fair question and no, I am not saying that. As far as the Gospel writers were concerned, the miracles of Christ were dramatic seals of authenticity and inexplicable displays of the power of God. They were performed to attest to the presence of the kingdom of God in this time and place. Nevertheless, I believe Jesus was able to make use of reframing strategies to initiate yet greater changes in the people he was healing.

Reframing by a slight shift in the people's worlds

Sometimes rather than giving an authoritative prescription, you can reframe someone's understanding by simply employing a slight shift in their world. Often the slightest word or action can have remarkable effects, like a small pebble thrown into a placid lake. Erickson's advice to the couple to change their schedule by thirty minutes is an example. So is Jesus' approach to the lame man.

Another is what I call the "occasional comment." I have a friend who is a clergyman. He was having regular contact with a member of his parish whose marriage was on the rocks. This man would come to the minister weekly to grumble and complain about his wife. At first my friend tried to get him to see the good things in her, to little avail. Next, he tried to discourage him from being so hard on her, again to no avail. Finally one day, the husband said, "Look, I hope you don't mind me coming around and bitching about my wife all the time." To which the minister replied, "Oh no, I hate her as much as you do!"

The man was mortified. He didn't hate his wife. And he wouldn't dare allow anyone else to hate her. But by exaggerating the man's position and by aligning himself with it, my friend was able to radically reframe the situation. It was that single, occasional comment which finally broke through.

I have read another story somewhere about a British colonel's wife in India during the British Raj. She was having a luncheon one day with all her aristocratic lady friends and was eager to impress them. However, her manservant had not arrived that morning as usual. The front stairs were littered with leaves and dust and she was frantic that the guests might arrive before the servant had swept them. When he finally did race in much later that normal, she was furious.

"I beg your pardon, Ma'am," the servant began. "I am sorry I am late, but my son died last night and we had to bury him this morning."

With that one statement he totally reframed her perception of him. Up till then, she saw him merely as a functionary who fulfilled a particular service for her. She didn't imagine his having a life or identity beyond his role as a servant. He was just the man who swept her front stairs for her. His one statement jarred her with the notion that he was a human being who felt grief and pain like anyone else.

This is the impact of a well-spoken occasional comment. But the occasional comment needn't necessarily even be a spoken word. Sometimes a new dynamic in a situation can fulfill the same function. And this new dynamic can be the tiniest change. A psychiatrist in a hospital for the mentally ill once took over a new ward and made one seemingly insignificant change: he installed a mirror in the center of the room. This was quite a departure from policy because this was a chronic ward and many of the patients had been there for decades. It had been assumed that a mirror or any other glass furnishing might pose a threat to the patients. These people had not looked at a mirror for up to thirty years!

The impact was sensational. Far from being harmful to them, it transformed the small community of patients. They approached the strange object cautiously at first. Then, having seen their reflection for the first time in many years, the began to look discerningly at themselves. The shock of their haggard and unkempt appearance prompted them to ask for toiletries, combs, and razors. Their appearances were dramatically changed and they became more alert and active.

Reframing as the work of a fool

The ministry of reframing is the surprising, simplistic, open, honest, naive ministry of the fool. Its simplicity and openness, its honesty and naiveté are its most appealing features—and yet beneath the surface of its disarming style the ministry of the fool institutes the kind of change that other approaches invariably fail to create:

Only a fool could see something useful in the normally infuriating trait of stubbornness and advise a friend to use that trait wisely.

Only a fool could see dirty, footprinted carpet as a symbol of a full, loving community of family and friends.

Only a fool could tell someone suffering from depression that he is the most depressing person he has ever met in order to help overcome that depression.

Only a fool would dare tell someone wanting to lose weight to put on weight.

Only a fool could advise a suicidal woman to give away flowers in order to find purpose in her life.

Only a fool thinks that you can save your marriage by changing your schedule by thirty minutes.

Only a fool can tell his friend that he hates the friend's wife in order to force him to see a better way forward.

And only a fool thinks that you can initiate a major change in the attitudes of the mentally ill by providing them with a mirror!

Can you see the dramatic and decisive impact that the ministry of the fool can have in creating significant changes in the lives of those he encounters? No doubt you can see how creative and ingenious a fool needs to be in order to reframe events or beliefs for others.

Hopefully, you are beginning to see that calling Jesus a fool actually implies that he had remarkable insight and a radical, unmistakable style. I believe him to have been a man of superior intellect who was able to cloak the impact of his wisdom with a freshness and naiveté that disarmed those he encountered.

If you tell two brawling individuals that just changing their daily regimen by thirty minutes each day will save their marriage, you appear so simplistic as to diffuse the anger, the resentment, the negative energy inherent in the relationship. By reading the Gospel accounts of Jesus' life and teaching, you will find him doing just that. He stalks, disarms, and seduces those around him and institutes radical, significant change.

Nothing thrills me more than when someone says to me, "I've never seen it that way before." As a theological lecturer, I find myself having to reframe my students' perceptions about religion and church, about God and faith, about worship and doubt time and time again. I think it was no different in Jesus' day. Most people had lost touch with their religious heritage. They were running out of faith and tired with theological controversy. The ecclesiastical system in place didn't seem to have anything useful to contribute to their struggle with daily living. They felt the religious leadership had become self-interested and out of touch. And yet their religion as it had originated had a lot to contribute to daily life. What they needed was a reframe. They needed to encounter their faith from a new perspective, one that made sense of their lives. Jesus the fool provided that very reframe. And he did so in such a wonderful and creative way as to have an impact on the world today.

Isn't it ironic that the new frame he offered this world has grown tarnished and dust-covered for lack of handling? Today, we need to see the reframe as he offered it. We don't need yet another frame (as some are suggesting). We just need to rediscover the perspectives and the insights Jesus brought to us. We need to get the picture reframed by the great Fool all over again.

As I mentioned earlier, the Gospel written by Luke is constructed in such a way as to put Jesus and his band of troubadours on the road to Jerusalem (and Jesus' imminent destruction). Like John Bunyan's Christian traveling to the Celestial City or J. R. R. Tolkien's hobbit journeying through Middle Earth, Jesus and his disciples hit the road bound for tragedy and the ultimate victory. They encountered a host of inquirers and fended off a bevy of detractors. They engaged in a series of adventures and even some misadventures. All the while, Jesus was continually reframing the perceptions of both friend and foe. We have looked at a number of contemporary examples of reframing. But if you have the stomach for it, we can join Jesus on the road and watch him delicately and deftly transforming the world around him. Who knows, he may even reframe some of our long-held perceptions along the way.

JESUS REFRAMES OUR BROKENNESS

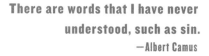

Luke 10:25–37

> There are words that I have never
> understood, such as sin.
> —Albert Camus

Our journey with Jesus the fool begins with our looking at the way in which he sought to reframe his contemporaries' perception of sin and guilt. In his day, as in ours, sin has been boiled down to mean simply the contravention of a particular set of rules or laws. Those laws had been summarized by the Decalogue, known to us today as the Ten Commandments; to sin was to break one or other of these rules. In other words, if you hadn't committed murder, adultery, or grand theft, then you hadn't sinned! But watch Jesus reframe the law to mean something quite different.

Jesus and the Jewish lawyer

In Luke 10:25–37 we find a story in which Jesus reframes the perception of a Jewish lawyer. The expert in Hebrew law asks Jesus, "Teacher, what must I do to inherit eternal life?" This might not seem to be such an unreasonable request of the man who claimed to be the resurrection and the life. After all, didn't Jesus himself claim he had the words of eternity? Wasn't it he who went so far as to say that whoever believed in him would never die? So to ask of him some specifics doesn't seem altogether out of place. Once posed, the questions about eternal life and the questioner provide Jesus the neatest possible opportunity to reframe his listeners' perceptions regarding true spirituality. The questioner was not some simple soul in search of truth. He was a prince of the religious system in place in first-century Israel. He was an expert in the Law, a rabbi, a scholar and ecclesiastical leader. He is attempting to engage his fellow teacher in some obtuse theological discussion. But for Jesus it is too great an opportunity to let go. And Jesus responds in fine dramatic form.

"Why do you ask me?" Jesus asks in overblown incredulity (verse 26). "What does the Law say? You are an expert in the Law of Moses. What does it say? What is it you teach the catechists at synagogue regarding finding favor with God?"

By turning the inquiry on the inquirer, he initiated a discussion with the rabbi that forced him to pursue the logical outcome of his own religious schema, to see its shortcomings, to be dumbfounded by its illegitimacy. This is the fool at his most devastating—leading his questioner down the avenue of his dreams only to encounter the dead end that has always been there, but which needed a guide to reveal it. As we see it unfold, you will watch Jesus bring about a powerful polarity response.

The lawyer, taken aback for a moment but forced now to think for himself, scratched his chin and mused, "Well, let me see. The most succinct form of the Law is the catechism that says, 'You must love the Lord your God . . . with all your heart and with all your strength and with all your soul.'" Pausing for a moment, he caught himself and with greater confidence he rehearsed the rest of the catechism, "And you must love your neighbor as yourself."

"Well," laughed Jesus, "so you knew the answer all along!" The sting of his sarcasm would not have been lost on the rabbi, but it is in fact his next comment which is his most radical. "Do this, fulfill the Law of Moses, and you will indeed live forever."

What Jesus did, like any decent satirist, was to adopt the schema, the mindset, of those he was criticizing in order to reveal their folly. Only by taking the rabbi and his fundamentalist legalism seriously could he show it for what it really was. Fulfill the Law of Moses and you will be saved. Live a life slavishly devoted to legalism, to religious piety based solely on your own efforts, and you will earn eternity. This, in fact, was so opposed to all that Jesus taught that those who knew him must have smelled a rat. But not the rabbi. He backed up for more, as Jesus must have surely known he would.

"Well, 'love your neighbor as yourself' might mean any one of a number of things," said the rabbi. "I have heard several of the great rabbinical interpretations. What would yours be? If I am to love my neighbor in order to find favor with God, who then is my neighbor?" Jesus' response was nothing short of masterful.

"I'll tell you a story," he said gently. "A man was going down from Jerusalem to Jericho. I don't need to tell you, rabbi, how treacherous a trip he was making. And alone! Well, as you can expect, he was set upon by thieves and beaten to within an inch of his life. They stole all he had—his robe, his sandals, everything. He lay naked and bloodied in the dust by the road—as good as dead. A priest came by, hurrying for fear of attack and, seeing the naked body by the road, glanced this way and that. He may have suspected a trap. Or he may have thought him already dead. Who can say? Nevertheless, he hurried by. Later a Levite happened along. He, too, was fearful and dared not dillydally on so dangerous a journey. These were not bad men, mind you, rabbi. Just frightened—as you or I would be!

"Then, some time later, a Samaritan happened along. Do I need to tell you, rabbi, how much we Jews despise the Samaritan dogs, and they us? No. Of course not. Anyway, the surprise here is that the Samaritan risked his life by stopping, by rolling the man over and discovering that he was hovering between life and death. It was the Samaritan who covered his nakedness, dressed his wounds, mounted him on his donkey and took him to the nearest inn. There, he paid in advance the man's board and medical expenses until his full recovery.

"I see you scoffing, rabbi. It is true that it is too great an act of mercy to believe, especially of a Samaritan, but give me some licence. If it were true, which of the three men who encountered the beaten man on the road was a neighbor to him?" Jesus leaned forward awaiting with interest the rabbi's response. And, of course, there could be only one response. The most obvious one. The rabbi no doubt felt the uneasiness of not knowing what Jesus was going to make of his answer, but not being able to second-guess him he responded sensibly, "Why, the one who had mercy on him."

"Indeed," Jesus said earnestly. "Go and do likewise." And with that their discussion came to a close and Jesus moved slowly away from the rabbi.

The impact of their exchange was yet to hit. Like a slow release drug, the realization of the dead end into which he had just been led dawned on the rabbi later, powerfully. Left alone and dazed by Jesus' story, he struggled to make sense of what had just gone on. Thinking deliberately, logically, sequentially, he retraced their steps.

"I asked him what I must do to live forever," the rabbi thought, "and he agreed that I must love my neighbor to gain eternal life. Then I asked him who was my neighbor, and he told a story in which my neighbor is everyone I encounter with a need. So, if I want eternal life, I must meet the needs of everyone I come across." And with that the true genius of Jesus can be observed. He agreed with the legalist that to find favor with a perfect God one must behave perfectly, then he introduced him to the implications of doing so. If to live perfectly is to love your neighbor, then that cannot be confined to your friends, your relations, those you like, but rather it must spill over to include everyone we encounter.

If true love demands selfless care and concern for our circle of relationships, it demands equally for those outside that circle. The parable of the Samaritan lays bare the implications of loving your neighbor. It involves great risk, great cost, great sacrifice. Imagine the hapless rabbi encountering his own theological position in all its depth for the first time: "If I would find God's favor and live forever, I must love my neighbor. That is, I must actively seek to meet the needs of every person I encounter. Why, that's impossible, I cannot even begin to meet all the needs of my immediate family. I cannot even begin to meet all the needs of my close friends, let alone every person I meet. I simply don't have enough time, enough energy, enough motivation, enough care, enough love. It would be physically and emotionally beyond my capacity to do so. It's *impossible!*"

And as Jesus moved off in the distance, it would be entirely appropriate to picture his wry smile and to watch him nod gently as he responded simply, "Right!"—for that is the very point of the parable. The so-called Good Samaritan is not just a symbol of doing good to others, as we have turned him into. He is a symbol to us of our despair, our hopelessness. When we observe his ridiculous, unbelievable, laughable act of grace and hear Jesus say, "Go and do likewise," we are bound to cry out, "It's impossible!!" And Jesus' response, wry and calculated, is simply, "Right." That's the point.

Jesus the fool took the rabbi, and us with him, to the ultimate conclusions of those theological systems that prescribe some way of earning God's favor. He allows us to see for ourselves the shortcomings of such an endeavor. He anticipates that our response to his story will be not a deepened resolve to go and love our neighbors more but rather a plaintive gasp, "That's impossible." That's the power of Jesus' foolishness. He displays our folly for all its worth. He buys into the systems of thought that we hold dear just long enough to expose their stupidity.

I recall hearing Walter Martin do precisely the same thing once when addressing an assembly made up predominately of Mormons. Martin had challenged the Mormon doctrine that held that God is merely an exalted man and a member of the audience rose to challenge him.

"Might I be allowed to prove to you," the young Mormon began, "from your own Bible that God is only a man exalted to the heavenly realms?"

Walter Martin asserted that if the young man could prove it from the Bible, he would be obliged to concede the Mormon's position. And so with that the gentleman proceeded to take Martin through a great list of texts. The eyes of the Lord are upon Israel (Deuteronomy 11:12), so God must have eyes. Jacob saw God face to face (Genesis 32:30), so God must have a face. The Psalmist committed his spirit to God's hands (Psalm 31:5), so God must have hands. Paul claimed that God had put all things under his feet (Ephesians 1:22)—and so it went on. This great list of body parts attributed to God was rehearsed as if proving that God was once a man.

Walter Martin, not unlike Jesus in the episode we have just observed, played along with great aplomb, nodding, and agreeing as each item was recalled. "Mmmm," he would reply solemnly at various intervals, "I see."

When the young man had finished, Martin responded. "I see your point, sir. In fact while you were reading, several other texts came to mind that also support your argument." The Mormon glared skeptically at him. Martin went on, "Look up Psalm 91:4 and read it aloud as you read those other verses."

With caution, the young man found the text and read it reluctantly: "God will cover you with his feathers and under his wings you will find refuge."

"So," responded Walter Martin, "what have we, then? Is God an exalted *chicken?*"

Foolish grace

It is a powerful tool to be able to engage in the machinations of another schema in order to highlight their fallacies. However, we need to be aware that Jesus' intention in this episode is not to scorn

Judaism as a whole. It was Jesus who claimed to have come not to destroy Judaistic hope but to fulfill it. Rather, he sought to display the self-righteousness of fundamentalism of some Jewish thinking for what it was. He mocked Jewish legalism by inviting the legalist to laugh at it himself and, in doing so, scorned all religious legalism that binds and detains its adherents.

So, what is he saying? God cannot be bought. That's it. That is his basic theological agenda. Human beings by their very nature cannot hope to impress God by their ability to jump through various legal hoops. And in making this point, Jesus harked back to a struggle that had beset Israel since Moses led them through the wilderness: the struggle between an allegiance to a contractual theology or to a covenantal theology.

Contractual theology describes a way of relating to a god based on a pact or contract, into which both parties enter, fully aware of the terms of that contract. The terms are expressed with the contractual formula, "If I do A, B, and C, you must do E, F, and G." In the case of religion, it is often expressed as, "If I pray so many times a day and sacrifice so many goats a week, my god must make my land fertile and protect me from natural disaster." When ill-fortune strikes, the terms of the contract dictate that you must have failed to pray hard enough or sacrifice correctly enough to impress your god. It is considered faithless to blame the deity for not coming through on the arrangement. Remember poor old Job?

The great ideal of Judaism is, in fact, a rejection of contractual theology, even though Israel drifted into and out of it at various points in her history. Judaism, rather, held to a covenant relationship with their God. Distinct from a contract formula, a covenant relationship—not unlike our marriage covenants—is a commitment between two parties based on love and devotion. Even when Israel drifts into open disobedience, God remains faithful, ever committed to the covenant he made with her. Even when he allows misfortune to occur it is as an act of devotion, an expression of fatherly discipline. Indeed, during the Babylonian Exile he doesn't turn his back on their covenant but continues to reveal his grace to Israel. In the Mosaic covenant, God and his people enter into a kind of marriage, as it were. And for God it is for life. It is an expression of grace, a theme Jesus returns to again and again. Indeed it is one of his most foolish ideas!

But the idea of grace is embedded right throughout the Hebrew scriptures. It is delightfully sketched for us in the powerful message of the Jewish prophet, Hosea. God once said to Hosea, "Hosea, I want you to marry a whore." Now, not being one to question the great God of the universe, Hosea complied and married a prostitute named Gomer. She had a child with him; she had another child with someone else; and she had yet another child with someone else. Before Hosea knew it, she was gone.

The God said to Hosea, "Hosea, where is your wife?"

And Hosea replied, "Where is my wife? She has deserted me, O Lord. She stands down at the pagan temple as a fertility object. The pagans come and have intercourse with her in the temple in order to incite their gods to send rain or make their cattle fertile. She is naked and humiliated and abused, a living testimony to my shame."

And God said to Hosea, "Hosea, I want you to go and buy your wife back." So with what little money he had, Hosea went to the temple and paid the cultic priest to buy his wife out of slavery for fifteen shekels and a handful of barley. When he got her home, God asked him, "Hosea, how do you feel?"

"How do I feel, Lord?" Hosea grinned. "I have the woman I love in my home, in my arms, in my bed and I feel fantastic. I just feel terrific."

And God said to Hosea. "Hosea, go and tell the people that that's exactly how I feel."

At the heart of Israel's faith was an allegiance to a God who had entered into a covenant with his people. He was the steadfast God, the loyal God, the faithful husband who, no matter how far his people strayed, would buy them back in an instant. G. K. Chesterton rightly said, "Let your religion be less of a theory and more of a love affair." The essence of covenant is love—not an external contract, but selfless, devoted love. I don't love my children because they bring home a good report card from school. I love them because they are my children.

That the rabbis and experts in the Law had turned God into a capricious deity who seemed to wait with anticipation for his people to fall and break the Law in order to break off relations with them was a perversion of the truth. A lurking vindictive God who wrings his hands at our every failure is a cruel and mistaken caricature. This is the very point the parable of the Good Samaritan makes. By highlighting how impossible it is for us to impress God by our ability to keep up our end of the bargain, it creates in us a yearning for another way.

The apostle Paul affirms this yearning, albeit far less creatively than did Jesus, when he says in Romans 3:23 that we are all sinners. In fact, the first three chapters of that letter are a detailed and systematic demonstration of human inadequacy. Sin is a biblical term, much abused, which simply means falling short of the mark. It, like many Bible words, relies on a mental image to convey its meaning. The image the word "sin" is meant to conjure is one of a marksman continually firing his arrow short of the target. When a marksman continually fires short, it means one thing:: he is too far from the mark. Sin means we are too far from God's glory to emulate his perfection on earth. This, in fact, is the key message of the Good Samaritan; we all fall short of the mark, no matter how hard we try.

Unfortunately, too much fire-and-brimstone-style preaching on sin has done nothing but dilute its impact on congregations today. Jesus the jester tells a story that allows our desperate inadequacy to sneak up on us. The apostle Paul simply comes out with it in the statement: "All have sinned," but Jesus allows its impact to dawn slowly, potently. Sadly, today we are often wary of people reminding us of our inadequacy. But it is on this very point that Christianity is at its most realistic. The way of Jesus approaches the realities of sin, evil, and guilt more closely than other major religions inasmuch as it has both good news and bad news. And yet they are both *real* news.

Jesus and Paul in their own ways remind us that we miss the mark. A cornerstone of Christian theology is that we need to feel bad about our inadequacy. St. Teresa of Avila said, "If you can serenely bear the trial of being displeasing to yourself, then you will be a pleasant place of shelter for Jesus." This is what it means to be a Christian. You cannot be a Christian unless you know what it is to be displeasing to yourself. This is the bad news. We cannot love well enough. We cannot serve well enough. We cannot act justly enough. We cannot love mercy enough. In spite of what many positive thinking teachers tell us, our experience reminds us that we are continually displeasing to ourselves. The good news that Jesus brought us is that if we confess our sins with contrition then our sins are forgiven. And forgotten.

It reminds me of the story of the American missionary priest working in the Philippines. When studying at seminary in the US, he had committed a sin of which he was deeply ashamed. Overwhelmed by guilt, he confessed his sin before his God and rested in the knowledge that God can be trusted to forgive us our sins and to wash us of our unrighteousness. But sadly, he did not rest for long. The nagging sense of guilt and shame had continued to linger with him. Upon arriving in the Philippines to begin his missionary service, he was approached by a young girl, a member of his parish, who claimed to have visions of the resurrected Christ.

The girl told him that Christ would appear at the foot of her bed every night. In fact, many members of the town were hearing of these visitations and asking her to inquire of Christ on their behalf. The missionary was skeptical of the visions, but considered them harmless as long as they remained part of the girl's personal spiritual experience. But since they were now inflaming the community, he felt he needed to act. After all, the church couldn't afford to have any unauthorized saints running loose, especially in his parish.

Upon investigation, the priest, deeply impressed with the girl's innocence and inner strength, could find nothing to indicate she was lying. On the other hand, he found nothing to prove that she wasn't a fraud. He determined to undertake the least sophisticated course of action. He would ask her a question that only Christ could answer. If she responded correctly, there would be very real cause to believe her.

There was, of course, one question that came to his mind immediately. If the girl was to inquire of Christ what sin it was that her priest had committed in seminary in America, this would be a true test of her legitimacy. The priest had never told a soul of his misdemeanor. He had confessed it to Christ and no one else. Certainly, no one in the Philippines could possibly know of it. If the girl discovered the correct answer to this question, the missionary believed that only Christ could have revealed it to her.

He posed the experiment to the girl. She seemed not the least perturbed, saying that many in her village asked of Christ all manner of questions. This one should not pose any great difficulty for Christ, she said. Then, demonstrating a maturity beyond her years, she dared ask her priest a question: "Does this sin still trouble you?" she smiled.

"It does. Greatly," the American replied solemnly.

"You have confessed it to Christ?"

"Of course, my child. That is why I want you to ask this question of him. It is something that only he has heard."

"Then," she ventured cautiously, "why does it trouble you? The Bible says that when we confess our sin, God casts it from his memory as far as the east is from the west."

The missionary nodded absently. He knew this better than she, he suspected. But he could not share her childlike, innocent faith in a God who not only forgives, but completely forgets. Several days later the girl met with her priest again.

"Did you ask Christ the question?" he asked her.

"I did, Father."

"And did he answer you?"

"He did."

Hesitantly, he inquired further, "You asked what sin it was I committed in seminary all those years ago?"

"Yes, Father, I did."

"And what did he say?"

"He said he couldn't remember."

And with that he wept before her as he would in the presence of any saint.

The painful truth

The Good Samaritan story is designed to lay bear our inadequacy, our sin, to remind us subtly that we are and always will be displeasing to ourselves. And yet this must be seen in the context of the whole message of Jesus, which is that when we confess our sins to God with contrition, he forgives us of them. He forgets them. This is the good news. But we must confess with contrition. Though not a term in popular usage, contrition is feeling badly about your sin. It is a temporary loss of self-esteem. Those who read Jesus' parable of the Samaritan accurately recognize that it was designed to heighten our contrition. It was designed to hit at the heart of our self-righteous formulas. The Samaritan ought to make us feel badly about how far short of the mark we fall.

Contrition hurts. It is painful. It is as simple as that. And we are a culture programmed to minimize discomfort. But contrition is a God-given corrective mechanism, built in for our own good. The truly evil ones in our world are those who have refused to bear the pain of contrition. When we burn our hand on a hot pan on the stove, we rant and rave and curse and swear at the pain, but we don't ever wish that heat didn't hurt. We recognize that our sense of touch, our ability to feel pain, is a corrective device built in for our own good.

Likewise with contrition. If we want to live in a community that feels no contrition, no guilt, then we might find such a community in, say, a maximum security prison. Though contrition hurts, we must never wish for a world without it. It is necessary to feel bad about oneself every so often.

Recently at a conference of business executives, a questionnaire was distributed that included the directive, "List all those things about yourself with which you are not pleased." Every response, without fail, listed such things as "I would like to move to the country," or "I wish I was happily married," or "I wish I was not married," or "I need to get a new car," or "I need to spend more time with the kids." In each case, these are not things about the executives themselves at all. Rather, they are things about their circumstances with which they are not happy. When this was pointed out to the group, the universal response was that these men and women belonged to a culture (the business culture) that strongly discouraged negative self image among its members. They were simply not used to being encouraged to be unhappy about themselves. This is not unique to executives. We are all victims of the "no regrets" mentality of our age.

Jesus rather radically suggests that temporary losses of self-esteem are not such a bad thing. To be aware of one's inadequacy with a contrite spirit is a wholly therapeutic experience. However, contrition is only self-correcting in the context of a keen sense of personal worth. For while it is necessary to feel contrite, it is also important that we love ourselves at all times. We must perceive our own value. In the context of healthy self-love, contrition maintains our balance and corrects against self-righteousness and arrogance. This is what Jesus calls us to: balance. If our guilt overwhelms us and turns into a denial of our own worth, we refuse to believe that God could forgive us. This is one of the most realistic aspects of Christianity. It affirms that we are sinners, unable to live up to our own (or God's) expectations. And on the other hand, it invests human beings with enormous value. The balance between contrition and self-love is the tension that the Gospel embraces with a robust vigor.

Real evil is the refusal to embrace that tension. It manifests itself in two forms. The first, already observed, is the arrogant refusal to bear the pain of contrition. The other form of evil is the refusal to believe that we are valued so highly by God as to be forgiven. There is nothing that holds us back more than our sense of unimportance. It is not true that only a select few people in history have the mark of greatness and that the rest of us are the flotsam and jetsam, the riffraff of humanity, whose primary purpose is to observe the greatness of others. Granted, Walt Disney, Adolf Hitler, Gandhi, and Martin Luther have left their mark on history, but so have we all. In every relationship, every conversation, every thought, every act, we contribute to culture. We are important. We are deeply valuable, the denial of which has led to the most atrocious destruction.

To return to Hosea, his life began to personify the yearnings and desires of God. This is a classic literary or artistic device. Earlier I mentioned the film *Jesus of Montreal* directed by Denys Arcand. It tells the story of a young actor named Daniel who is commissioned by the Catholic Church in Montreal to write and produce a new contemporary version of a passion play. Daniel's research and his obsession with Christ's life and death begin to permeate his thinking to such a degree that various episodes in his own life begin to mirror the life of Christ. In a creative way, Jesus is brought into twentieth-century Canada and the audience is invited to view how twentieth-century Canada might have really treated Christ if he came to them.

Hosea does exactly the same thing. The prophet plays the role of God, and his wife, Gomer, plays the role of God's people. As we saw before, the great function of the story is to rehearse that fact that God is like a faithful, devoted husband who would take his faithless wife back at any time. By buying his wife back out of slavery in a contractual religion (as the pagan fertility cults certainly were), Hosea demonstrates the value God places on his people. Here is the remarkable tension between contrition and self-love. Even though his people are faithless, naked, and humiliated, God considers them worthy of buying back. The reaction the prophet would have been seeking from the people was twofold: first, the shame of seeing oneself represented as a whore; and second, the dignity of glimpsing the value God places on us.

Picture the scene when Hosea finally got his whore-wife home from the pagan temple. Imagine him taking her to his bed and her refusing him. "No, no," she might cry, covering her face with her hands, "I am unworthy. How could you make love to me? I am filthy. You deserve so much better."

In a very real sense, the parable of the Good Samaritan simply affirms our unworthiness. Our unworthiness needs to be affirmed. A man comes to Jesus asking to what formula he must subscribe in order to find God's favor. Jesus tells him to subscribe to the very rigor to which he was already committed and then illustrates to him that the only real benefit of that rigor is to highlight his hopeless inability to earn God's favor at all.

Jesus has now totally reframed the Law. Where it was once seen as a means of salvation, it now becomes the barometer of how unworthy we are of such salvation. But the Gospel of Jesus is that in the context of our unworthiness, God still considers us lovable. The message of Jesus is that we are loved beyond our wildest imagining.

JESUS REFRAMES FORGIVENESS

king christ the world is all aleak; and
life preservers there are none
—e e cummings

f laws like the Ten Commandment serve only to remind us of our terrible inadequacy, what hope is there for the human race? The answer is that Jesus also reframes how we find a way out of our impasse and it is not through an increased commitment to some external set of regulations. In this regard, Jesus is running contrary to every belief in the Ancient Near East, whether educated or not, that religion is the regimen by which we purchase the deity's good graces. For Jesus, religion is an expression of devotion to a deity who has already bestowed his good graces upon his people. Watch carefully and see how cleverly he accomplishes this.

Jesus and a repentant woman

In Luke 7:36–39 we find the following disturbing story. Jesus had been invited to the home of a Pharisee named Simon, one of the conservative religious leaders of the Jewish community. This was no ordinary social gathering; Jesus' reputation was growing and he was beginning to be perceived by the common people as a champion of their cause, a religious teacher who spoke the language of the street, who gave their faith some practical application, thus making sense of the relationship between religion and daily life.

The Pharisees, on the other hand, were revered, even feared, as men of unattainable holiness, keepers of the ancient traditions, separated, disconnected, and esoteric. They were the orthodox guardians of the faith. To them, Jesus would have been disdained in the way some academic theologians today might disdain popular Christian literature or in the same way professors of psychology might pooh-pooh many of the self-help books currently available.

Jesus did not share their training, their heritage, their general concerns. He was certainly literate (and many in his society would not have been), but for the most part he was not formally educated in theology. He taught with word pictures. He associated with common people. He came from Nazareth. He was unconcerned with minute and specific interpretations of the Torah or with the teaching of the priests. Jesus was, to the Pharisees, a pop teacher, useful only insofar as he supported the concerns of the Pharisaic community.

Jesus was potentially quite dangerous to the religious authorities. If a group's power is derived from mystery, from fear and uncertainty, from its role as a custodian of ancient secrets, then nothing strips that power more effectively than the shedding of the hard light of day on its esoteric machinations. If Jesus was making Jewish religion more accessible, if he was making the Law more sensible, then he was undermining the degree to which the Pharisees could maintain their mystique. In fact, towards the end of his short life, the Pharisees had secretly declared out and out war against him. They began, however, by expressing their contempt for him far more civilly. They began with dinner invitations to "discuss" with Jesus his uncommon approach. Invariably, these were really intended to be opportunities to humiliate and embarrass him. And invariably, Jesus' sense of the moment triumphed magnificently.

We must be aware of the type of world Jesus was entering when he accepted such invitations. The Pharisee had committed himself to a life of holiness, of separation from all things impure. However, unlike the Christian monks centuries later who remained holy by physically separating themselves from the world in monasteries and heritages, the Pharisees expressed their distinction from impurity through an arduous allegiance to ritual purity rules. They ate their meals with the general community, but did so only after ritual cleansings had been completed. In this way they remained an example to the community of what real holiness looked like; they were to have nothing to do with impure food or impure people.

Their conduct at meals was also to be an example to the community. They were not given to carousing, coarse language or frivolous discussion. In fact, they often formed religious societies, and engaged in religious debates over meals. Often a visiting teacher or notable thinker was invited to speak. So you can see how it would not be unusual for a man of Jesus' increasing popularity to be asked to the home of a Pharisee like Simon.

In Luke's account of the event so much is assumed by him and not explicitly mentioned that we, who are not Middle Easterners, miss much of what is really happening. Luke refers to Jesus accepting the invitation and "reclining," verse 36, at Simon's house. The only meals at which people reclined were formal banquets that had precisely dictated traditional roles of guest and host. The gates and doors were always left open to allow anyone, including the uninvited, to enter. A guest, especially a rabbi or a notable person, would be greeted with a kiss and much fanfare. A long, low table was placed in the center of the meal room, and the great wooden dishes were arranged along it or sometimes simply on the floor.

The guests would recline on low couches around the table in order of rank, leaning on their left elbow with their feet turned away from the table. They would have removed their sandals at the door and servants standing behind the couches would pour large basins of water over their dust-covered feet and wipe them clean. Behind the servants members of the community would gather to observe the feast and eavesdrop on the conversation. They would not have been thought obtrusive for doing so, as the whole occasion was as much a community event as a private meal.

For a host to omit any detail of this ritual would have been unthinkable and a gross insult to the guest. In particular, washing the feet (unclean feet were a symbol of great unworthiness) and kissing the cheek were indispensable aspects of the banquet. To refuse to offer them would be to show contempt for your guest. H. B. Tristram, the intrepid nineteenth-century traveler, wrote how once in Tunis he was attending a formal banquet when his companion leaned over and whispered in his ear not to trust the host because he had not kissed them on entering. As it turned out, Tristram found that the advice was particularly perceptive.

When Jesus arrived at the home of Simon, he was not kissed, nor were his feet washed. Neither, in fact, was he anointed with oil. This later omission would have been less offensive than the other two, although anointing with oil was a reasonably common procedure. It is hard for us from our vantage point of less formalized Western culture to conceive of the affect of such a snub, thought we do have our traditional greeting customs which if avoided create offense. Imagine turning up at the home of someone who had invited you for a meal only to be greeted at the door without a handshake or kiss—no welcome, no invitation to enter, no offer of a drink or a seat, no introduction to the other guests there. It would be the height of rudeness. You simply wouldn't tolerate it.

Some people suggest that Simon's behavior was merely an oversight. And yet so basic to the very fabric of the Middle Eastern banquet were these pleasantries that to omit them must have been intentional. Simon's rebuff of Jesus was clearly calculated. He had invited the upstart rabbi from Nazareth to his dinner party precisely in order to humiliate him, to entice him into the cultured and elegant circles of the Establishment in order to scorn, mock, and embarrass him.

A guest might respond to such humiliation in one of two ways. First, he might express his outrage at such a snub. He could rant and rave and storm out of the banquet. However, this would have been unheard of in the Middle East. No matter how atrociously a guest was treated or how meager the food offered, one would never shame the host by mentioning one's dissatisfaction. Or second, the guest might silently endure the rebuff and later refuse any relations with the offending host. If Jesus took either course of action, Simon still expected to score points against him. If Jesus chose rage, Simon might thereafter recall his encounter with the young, hotheaded, arrogant rabbi. If Jesus chose submission, Simon had the whole night to demean and abuse him before everyone in the community.

It is a sad and pathetic character who seeks to build himself up at the expense of others. I remember attending a dinner party once and being seated next to a very loud man who became progressively louder the more alcohol he consumed. I asked him about himself and found out where he lived, what he did, what family he had. He was, like most people, more than happy to talk about himself. Then he turned to me and, as an afterthought, inquired as to what I did.

"I'm a minister. I work with a church," I said.

"A minister of religion?" he stuttered.

I nodded

"Well," he bellowed quite loudly, silencing several of the other conversations around the table, "how about that? A minister! This guy is a minister. You know I really admire you. I admire anyone who is trying to make this world a better place."

He was now speaking so loudly and commanding such attention with his gestures that virtually everyone was listening in. He continued.

"I do. I really admire you. You think you can change the world, don't you? Well you haven't got a hope in hell!"

At this everyone laughed at his gregarious display and he slammed me affectionately on the back. I smiled rather meekly, but

I was embarrassed by his put-down. Later, after the meal, he told me about his wayward son and asked if there anything I could do to help him. After making it very clear to everyone at the table that I was wasting my life in the ministry, he now asked for my assistance with his son. I resisted pointing this out to him and offered what advice I could. He went on to tell me of his strict Catholic upbringing and the great fear of religion that had been instilled in him. It made me think of the way we attack the things we fear. This was Simon's condition; he felt fear, insecurity, and uncertainty, and he took it out on Jesus.

As Jesus entered Simon's home, another face appeared. She was a whore, a woman of the street, another of the nameless destitutes who plied their trade in the city. She, like a handful of others, had gathered at the gate and watched the guests arrive. She had followed them to the doorway and stood respectfully at the rear of the small crowd as each guest was greeted by Simon the Pharisee. She joined the crowd, silent and obeisant, her vocation unmistakable. At some meals a prostitute might garner some business after the feats, but never at the home of a Pharisee.

But she had not come on business. She had come hoping to catch a moment with Jesus. She had heard him on the street. She had watched him as he spun his tales, as he blessed the poor and the helpless, as he had reinvested people with meaning and purpose. She had felt herself rising with a new sense of dignity and self-respect as she heard him teach about God's love and forgiveness. Every rabbi she had encountered had treated her with contempt. She had never dared look into the face of a Pharisee lest she incur the shame of his glare. Yet this rabbi, this one called Jesus, had once stared right at her across the crowd as she listened to him. This rabbi traveled in company with women, some of whom it was said had once been prostitutes. Jesus radiated a sense of acceptance and tolerance that had affected her deeply and somehow changed her inwardly.

She dared to hope for a moment to meet him, to thank him, to acknowledge him. She may not have been at all certain what she wanted, but she was driven by a desire to encounter him as one person to another. For her to desire this of any man, let alone a rabbi, had probably both surprised and thrilled her.

It had occurred to her that as a holy man this Jesus ought to be anointed, to be blessed as God's servant. She determined to offer him a gift to express her devotion to him. But so desperately poor was she that she had nothing to present to him. As a prostitute, she owned no property. She lived hand-to-mouth, owning only the clothes on her back. She did have a small flask shaped in the form of an alabaster jar that she hung on a leather thong around her neck. In it she had a cheap perfume that acted as a type of deodorant. You can imagine how important deodorant might be to a woman who spent her days lying under sweating men.

She offered to Jesus the symbol of her impurity. The flask was like the badge of her trade. To anoint Jesus' head with oil would have been reminiscent of the way in which priests were commissioned or the way kings were inaugurated. She felt either image was appropriate but, of course, she had no oil—and to touch the top of an important man's head was unheard of. So she determined to anoint his feet with her perfume. Surely, she thought, he would appreciate the significance of this act. Whether she herself fully realized the symbolism of her offering to Jesus the emblem of her past life (for surely she intended to join his community and live in the care of those who embraced his teaching of acceptance and mercy), we will never know. But the offering of her flask of perfume as an ointment to Jesus was an inspired idea.

And so she followed him, at a distance of course. Always cautious to move in the anonymity of the crowd, she waited for a time when there were few people around him. But now that Jesus had become so public a figure, she began to despair that any such moment would eventuate. When she heard that he was eating at the home of a Pharisee, she was certain this evening would not be hers. She would never do anything to draw attention to herself in the home of a religious man like Simon. Nevertheless, she followed him there in the desperate hope that perhaps after the banquet, on the street later after all had left, she might encounter him alone, or with only his supporters around him.

And so both Jesus and the whore arrived at Simon's together. And yet not together. She hung back and watched anxiously, and as she did, she observed the public spectacle of Simon's calculated humiliation of Jesus. With each stage in the ordered rebuff, first the absence of the kiss of greeting, then the refusal to wash his feet, then the seating of Jesus far from the host, she grew increasingly indignant. This, after all, was the man who had transformed her life by reinvesting her with dignity and self-respect. This man among men was being treated as if he was worth nothing more than a whore. She knew what it was like never to have had her feet washed. She knew how it felt to be treated as if you were worthless. And now, as she watched Jesus treated in this very manner, her indignation rose within her and turned to anger and her anger soon turned to rage.

Jesus, on the other hand, needed no affirmation of his personal worth from a fearful and deceitful Pharisee. Aware of the possibility of such a snub before he arrived, Jesus took the slight with characteristic grace. He remained silent and apparently unperturbed throughout the meal, though you can imagine the pain he might have felt at such treatment. The woman had positioned herself with the small gathering of onlookers behind where Jesus was reclining. She half-listened as Simon held forth about the Talmud, punctuating his lecture with witticisms and quaint tales. She could hardly pay him the attention he seemed to be demanding of those in the room. Her heart was filled with rage and her eyes with tears. Such humiliation was intolerable. She felt herself begin to quake with anger. How could they not even kiss him? How could they leave his feet filthy? How could they treat him like a dog?

Overwhelmed by the potent cocktail of devotion and gratitude and rage, she felt herself moving forward, breaking from the safety of the gathering. Looking back, she could never have imagined herself doing such a thing, but this was the evidence of her newfound dignity. In a sad and yet determined way, she tried to compensate for Simon's misdemeanor. He had refused Jesus a kiss, so she would kiss him. He had refused to wash to Jesus, so she would wash him. And yet having broken forth, she found herself in the glare of a group of men who perceived her with nothing but hostility. It was then that she realized her folly. How could she, a whore, kiss a rabbi on the cheek? This would have been hopelessly misconstrued and altogether out of the question. And yet she had committed herself to some action by breaking into the banquet.

Beset by confusion and sheer embarrassment, aware that every eye was now upon her, she threw herself at Jesus' dirty feet and began to kiss and kiss and kiss. Frantically she smothered his feet with her kisses, such was her gratitude and, as she showered this affection on him, she wept as she had never wept in her life. Her tears flowed as if a floodgate had been opened. From deep within her rose a tide of emotion, of release, of sheer joy, pouring forth like a torrent. By now she cared nothing of who saw her. This release was too great a blessing to allow shame to hold it back.

Simon sprang to his feet. Other guests jumped up in shock. As for Jesus, he could barely move as the woman clung to his legs, wailing like a baby. Tears and saliva would have run down his dusty feet, leaving behind tracks in the grime. He didn't know how to respond to her in this context. He sensed her devotion and realized her potential shame and placed a firm but gentle hand upon her back, accepting her adoration and sharing in her joy. He must have smiled broadly, so infectious was her happiness. At the other end of the room, Simon viewed this with some delight, though he feigned shock and outrage. Such a scene, he thought, only contributed to the general embarrassment of Jesus.

The woman, only half aware of her actions, so intoxicating was her gratitude, realized what a dreadful mess she was making and though of how she might retrieve the situation. Knowing that she had no towel to wipe down Jesus' feet, and recognizing that her dress was dusty from the street, she reached up and undid her loosely bound hair. It fell in long dark trusses from the top of her head and spilled across Jesus' feet. In a split second, she must have been aware that she had done the unthinkable and the gasps from the onlookers would have confirmed her fears. They thought she was seducing the rabbi from Nazareth.

For a woman to let down her hair in the Middle East is for her to initiate a sexual act. It was an intimate, tender gesture that a peasant woman only allowed her husband to observe. In fact, the Talmud suggests that a woman can be legally stoned for letting down her hair in the company of other men. Even today, in some strict Islamic cultures, male hairdressers are forbidden from working on women's hair for this very reason.

Of course, the woman at Simon's house had no husband. No one's honor had been offended. But the host had been outraged. For a whore to seduce a rabbi in the house of a Pharisee was scandalous. Simon would have no doubt seen to it that such an episode was well reported. Why, this Jesus didn't even spring to his feet. He didn't push her away. He didn't scowl in disgust at her lurid behavior. He simply lay there and allowed it to continue. In fact in Simon's eyes the rabbi's behavior was as scandalous as the woman's.

Aware now of her glaring indiscretion, the woman knew her time was short. Though she hadn't looked up, she must have been certain that Simon would be motioning for his servants to remove her from the room. Who knows what they might do with her? If she was lucky they would only throw her out on the street. It occurred to her that she must fulfill her intention now or never, while she still had a moment. Fumbling, she reached into her dress to remove the flask of perfume from between her breasts and, in so doing, exposed herself to those around the table. It was another gross indiscretion. The loosening of a women's hair and the uncovering of her breast were actions of a highly erotic nature. At the table of religious men, this was unheard of. Hastily, she poured the ointment on Jesus' feet and collapsed on the floor exhausted, humiliated, and frightened.

No words were spoken. In fact, it would have happened so fast that there would hardly have been time for words. From her first hesitant approach to Jesus, to her uncontrollable weeping, to the loosening of her hair and to the exposing of her bosom, it was one stupid gaffe after another. If she wasn't so pathetic a character, it might have been like an Abbott and Costello sketch. But she was pathetic, truly hopeless and abandoned.

Simon might have drawn some perverse pleasure from this outrageous scene. After all, if his intention was to undermine to credibility of the Nazarene rabbi, what better fodder than having a whore behave so sensually while draped around Jesus' legs? However, even Simon felt uncomfortable with her display. Pharisees were particularly conservative people. Such a display would surely have brought some disrepute to Simon's name and to his home. As host, he needed desperately to rescue the situation. He did so by shifting the focus away from himself, or even the woman, and laying shame upon Jesus. This was, after all, in keeping with his original intention.

The Pharisee engaged in what Shakespeare would call an aside. He scoffed arrogantly and charged Jesus with the indiscretion. "If this man really was a prophet," he said, "he would have known who and what sort of woman this is who is seducing him. She is a whore."

And here lies the very crux of the episode and the very point that Jesus would later make. You see, Jesus proved he was a prophet by the very fact that he *did* see who this woman was. He sensed her repentance. He felt her relief and knew her joy at being forgiven. It is Simon who saw nothing but an erotic act. This is partly what it is to be a prophet: to see things as God would see them. When Jesus looked at the woman's unbound hair, he saw devotion, gratitude, and repentance. When Simon saw the same thing, he perceived lust and licentiousness. Can you see the way two people can observe the very same drama, but respond differently given the distinct frames they place around the action?

In a church to which I once belonged, there was a young woman who was suffering at the hands of a very violent husband. Whenever she and her two children left him to return to her mother's home, he would chase her and retrieve them. He was brutally cruel to her. We advised her of her legal rights and made many resources available to her, including the offer of sanctuary in some of the homes of church people. But she refused to take advantage of these options, fearing her husband's response. It occurred to us that she was a young woman without dignity or self-respect. We remained open and supportive to her.

Then, one evening, after hearing a sermon on finding inner strength and new life in following Jesus, she responded to God's love. As she walked to the front of the church to express her new-found dignity, you could see her chest puffed up with respect and her face glowing with hope. She left her husband, refused to give in to the intimidation and threats and began a new life. She did so after years of struggle, but the element that tipped the scales was the dignity she realized she had after hearing Jesus' message of love.

I tell this story (a very happy one in the end) because on the evening that she walked barefoot down the aisle of our church, I looked up at our congregation as I held this sobbing young woman in my arms and prayed for her. Many people had looked up and their faces were beaming with the joy of what was happening to this woman. Later, some commented that it had been a most moving and entirely spiritual experience for them. However, some others commented that they were hoping that the next time she came to church she would wear shoes. They felt it irreverent to be barefoot in the house of God.

When some people looked at that woman they saw repentance, hope, joy, and new life. When others looked at her, they saw her bare feet. This is the difference between prophets and those whose religion is an excuse for insecurity. This is the difference between Jesus who accepted the prostitute's devotion and Simon who was reviled by it. The Pharisee desperately needed a reframe. He needed another way of seeing things. Jesus, the great reframer, is about to do just that and in no uncertain terms.

Jesus and an unrepentant Pharisee

In Luke 7:40–47 the story continues. Now at last Jesus, who was invited to this table to be made a fool of, began to play the fool with dramatic results. "I have something to say to you, Simon," he explained. It was a joke. It was a jester's tale. It was an unbelievable piece of absurdity, but one that would cut the Pharisee to the quick, take the situation out of his hands and reveal to all the depth of insight that Jesus possessed. It would decisively reframe the way Simon and the other guests saw the impact of true repentance and the power of God's forgiveness. And yet, as every good fool knows, only as a jest can many a true word be said.

"Two men owed money to a certain moneylender. One owed him five hundred denarii and the other owed him fifty. Neither of them could afford to repay him, so he canceled both their debts," Jesus said. How about that? He just canceled their debts. One was a greater debtor. The other not so great a debtor. And yet they were both leveled in their need. Neither could pay. So, treated as equals, their debts were equally canceled. Simon wondered what was coming next.

"Tell me, Simon, which of the two will love the moneylender more?" Jesus must have smiled with the all-knowing grin of the fool.

Simon sensed the insecurity of not knowing what would be made of his answer but had no choice but to play along by answering logically, "The one, I suppose, who had the larger debt canceled."

He was caught in a trap. The genteel and sophisticated banquet to which he had invited Jesus in order to humiliate him had turned into a farce—a tragic comedy of errors. Before him Jesus sat comforting a bereaved woman. There was perfume spilled about the floor and the other guests, at one minute repulsed and now intrigued, hung on every word, wondering what Jesus would make of this scene. Things had not proceeded as planned and now the pressure was all on Simon. It was he who was the fish out of water, not Jesus.

Now truly in command of the situation, Jesus behaved like the classic fool, preparing to say the things that no one else would dare to speak. In fact, he launched a tirade at the hapless Pharisee. "Do you see this woman?" he said sharply. Of course Simon could see her. She was lying prostate in the middle of his banqueting room. "I entered your house! And you gave me no water for my feet, but she wet my feet with her tears and wiped them with her hair. You refused me a kiss, but this woman, from the time I arrived, has not stopped kissing my feet. You did not put oil on my head, but she has poured perfume on my feet."

Jesus' behavior was nothing short of insolent. It was the height of rudeness for a guest to question the hospitality of his host. It was said that a proper guest said, "What trouble my host has gone to! And for all my sake!" while an evil host remarked, "Bah! What trouble he has caused!" The proper guest in the Middle East would always show appreciation for even the most meager offering. (I have a friend of Armenian descent from Baghdad who tried to give up drinking coffee. He told me it was impossible because whenever he went to his relatives' homes, they offered him their rich, black, strong brew. "Why don't you just refuse it?" I ignorantly asked, to which he simply shook his head.)

In our culture, a polite "No, thank you," might be quite acceptable. It might be all right to refuse to eat certain food served to you. But to the Middle Easterner, this was unthinkable. That Jesus dared to criticise the hospitality of the Pharisee was anathema. But Jesus ventured to do it in the guise of the jester. In the context of his cute story about the two debtors, he was able to apply its meaning to Simon's rudeness. And yet, what he had in mind was much more than a critique of Simon as a host. He had a far greater message than that.

"Therefore, I tell you," Jesus continued, his voice perhaps still crackling with an inflection of anger, "her sins, which were many, have been forgiven. So she loves much. But he who thinks he has little to be forgiven, loves little."

The target of his stinging attack was perfectly clear to all in attendance. After systematically comparing the virtues and oversights of the woman and the Pharisee respectively (a comparison with which no one could really argue), he returned to his parable about the two debtors and clearly demonstrated that the woman was like the debtor who owed a large sum. The clear inference was that Simon was like the man who owed the smaller sum. The most dramatic element of this reframe was the radical contention that they are *both* debtors! Sure, it may well be that the woman owed much more, but just like the two men in the story they were equally unable to repay their debt. Jesus' most cutting suggestion was that the Pharisee and the whore were leveled by their inability to repay their debt to God.

However, the Pharisee and the whore responded in entirely different ways. As Simon himself anticipated, the one who is forgiven more will express devotion much more than the one who feels he is forgiven less. The impact of Jesus' reframe must have hit Simon in four waves. First, it occurred to him that this rabbi from Nazareth was telling him that he, a Pharisee, was a sinner in debt to God. Second, this implied he was as equally unable to repay his debt to God as was a whore. Third, God in his grace, like the benefactor in the story, had canceled his debt—in other words, forgiven him of his sin—and God had just as graciously canceled the debt of the prostitute.

And fourth, if all this was true (and a Pharisee would never dare question the orthodoxy of such basic tenets of Jewish faith as sinfulness, grace, and forgiveness), then he ought to have been overjoyed by the prospect of forgiveness. In fact, whilst a prostitute might have been entitled to have been even more thrilled with her forgiveness because of her many sins, this ought not to have detracted from a Pharisee's sense of exultation that God had released him from his debt. The upshot of this four-stage realization of Jesus' message must have begged the question by Simon: "Why, then, do I not feel the same sense of devotion and adoration as this whore does?" The shattering answer is: "Because you are so conceited as to imagine yourself perfect."

The Fool has robbed the Pharisee of his delusion. He has snared him by throwing the cold, hard light of day on his own folly. He has simply taken the theological principles, to which Simon himself would have been committed, to their logical conclusion. Like the naive young boy who dares to cry out that the emperor has no clothes, Jesus dares to expose the naked conceit of the religious leader who thinks himself better than anyone else.

Indeed, it has been suggested that he told Simon the parable in order to reprove him for not wanting contact with sinners such as the woman. The damning conclusion would ring in the ears of a man like Simon: we are all sinners. Some may have lived more holy lives than others, but we are all in debt to God's grace and forgiveness, and to that end there is no one who can claim to be better, or more favored in God's sight, than others. In fact, in Jesus' economy of things, the greater sinners are afforded the greater forgiveness. This is a truth that can be terribly abused, as the apostle Paul pointed out ("What then, shall we go on sinning so that grace may increase? By no means!"[11]), but it is a truth nonetheless. And the more forgiven one feels, the more gratitude one wants to express.

The forgiven woman

In Luke 7:48–50 Jesus turned to the woman whom he had cradled in his arms. She had, perhaps, composed herself and was enjoying the rhythm of his embrace, as he held her close to his chest, his heart beating rapidly after his heated encounter with Simon. Looking into her face through eyes filled with love he announced in a firm and steady voice, "Your sins have been forgiven."

To this the woman registered no surprise. After all, it had been her commitment to the belief that she was forgiven that drove her to her desperate action of devotion. And here is the sting on the tale. I believe Jesus didn't forgive her her sins there on the floor of Simon's lounge room. He merely announced what she already knew.

This is a contentious point. Some Bible scholars believe that Jesus himself forgave her sins in some sacramental way there on the spot. However, if that was the case, it runs contrary to the whole point he was making in his parable. The story of the two debtors presupposes that the forgiveness of their debts was a supreme act of mercy, of grace on the part of the moneylender. The issue of gratitude and devotion arose as a *result* of the forgiveness. Jesus claimed that the woman's act of thanksgiving was in response to having her debt to God canceled. It would then appear contradictory for him to forgive her after that act. In fact, if he was forgiving her after the act, it would imply that you could earn God's forgiveness by costly acts of devotion. This would be the very opposite to the point Jesus had just made to Simon. It is extremely important that we recognize that Jesus was simply confirming for the woman what she knew all along. Your sins *have been* forgiven.

In other words, a life lived in costly devotion to God is a commitment most appropriately made *in response to God's grace, not in order to achieve it!* This is a fundamental stumbling block for many religious people. It was Simon's tragic and deluded belief that his life of ceremonial cleansings, his study of the Torah and Talmud, his offerings and sacrifices—his whole religious fervor, in fact—would impress God enough to earn his favor.

Jesus never condemns a strict religious lifestyle as long as it is engaged in as a result of an encounter with God. He never condemns

Pharisees, for example, because of their lifestyle of religious regulation. If such a lifestyle bespeaks the devotion and gratitude that one senses after experiencing God's grace, it is to be encouraged. But if it is a badge of office, a mark to show spiritual superiority, then it is roundly condemned by Jesus.

Jesus reframes of our ideas of forgiveness

Jesus turned theological presuppositions upside down. He reframed what was thought about forgiveness and redemption. In short, he claimed that there are two types of sin and two types of sinners. Simon sinned within the confines of religiosity. The woman sinned outside those confines. There is an old Yiddish proverb: "Better a sinner who knows he is a sinner, than a saint who knows he is a saint."

I was once preaching in a large, respectable Southern Baptist church in North Carolina. The minister went to great lengths to introduce me to the local senator, the mayor and police chief, all of whom were members of the church. I had been invited to preach every night for a week in this church and, sure enough, every night they all kept coming back for more. In the southern US, church is a real social event. Every night I was urged by the minister and the church leaders to "preach to the sinners." They prayed before each service that there would be some "sinners" in the congregation. And each night I was expected to preach God's forgiveness and mercy to "sinners."

I began to realize that what they meant by "sinners" was outsiders, those who were not regular worshippers in this church. Each night the members all turned out, wearing suits and ties and their Sunday best. And each night they hoped that some "sinners" might be touched by the message of Jesus' love.

On the second last evening of my stay with them, I felt constrained to speak about something altogether different: severed relationships; the need for people inside churches to exhibit love, compassion, and forgiveness both within their fellowships and to those outside. I told the story of what had happened at Simon the Pharisee's house and said that any church worthy of being named after Jesus ought to exhibit the same love as he did. I suggested that perhaps there were people in church who had an enmity between themselves and others that they had refused to resolve and that now was as good a time as any for those issues to be dealt with.

Every so often in the life of churches (as in the lives of individuals), new insights dawn quickly and dramatically. The timeless power of the Parable of the Two Debtors seemed to work its magic that night. It turned out that in the years and months before my visit there had been some bitter disputes and factional infighting in the church. Jesus' foolish story cut deeply into the hearts of church people who had held tightly to resentment and anger. People realized that "sinners" weren't just people who didn't go to their church. People realized that they themselves were as much in need of forgiveness as anyone.

Luke's story of what happened at Simon's house ends with the other guests gasping at the audacity of Jesus: "Who does he think he is, forgiving sins?" It is an entirely appropriate question given the circumstances. After the chaotic scene at the banquet, Simon and his guests are left with two options: belief or revulsion. Either this rabbi from Nazareth was a rude and impulsive young man who insulted his host's hospitality and dared to act like God by forgiving the sins of a salacious and uninvited whore, or he was truly God's agent of forgiveness. As the writer C. S. Lewis said, either Jesus is a liar, a lunatic, or he is Lord:

> I am here trying to prevent anyone from saying the really foolish thing that people often say about him: "I'm ready to accept Jesus as a great moral teacher, but I don't accept his claim to be God." That is the one thing we must not say. A man who was merely a man and said the sort of things Jesus said would not be a great moral teacher. He would either be a lunatic—on the level with the man who says he is a

poached egg—or else he would be the Devil of Hell. You must make your own choice. Either this man was, and is, the Son of God; or else a madman or something worse . . .[12]

If Jesus could not forgive the woman's sin, then his promise to do so is, as Lewis suggests, a monstrous deceit. In this episode Jesus, the great reframer, reverses the usual religious trend that sees the faithful performing acts of service in order to earn their God's forgiveness. Jesus in effect says, "if you respond to me with acts of devotion and worship, do so in light of my love and mercy, not in order to achieve them."

I know many well-meaning Christian people who treat prayer and Bible reading as acts of service, though it might seem strange. Prayer, reflection, and meditation are entirely appropriate ways of expressing your gratitude to God, as is the reading and study of the ancient books of faith collected in the Bible. However, many Christians feel compelled to pray and read the Bible out of some vain hope that in performing these acts of devotion, they will twist God's arm to grant them his favor. I have heard it expressed as, "Gee, I've been having a lousy week, and I know why. I haven't prayed or read my Bible lately." They then commit themselves to some program of daily devotions in order to rectify the reasons for their bad week, as if by performing these duties they can earn God's good graces. This was the very mistake for which Jesus condemned Simon.

By beginning our day with a time of prayer and study of the Bible, we shouldn't imagine we are guaranteeing for ourselves a divine blessing that will make everything sweet that day. In the same way, it is superstitious to imagine that when we neglect to pray and study we are risking having a bad time of it. Daily prayer and Bible study ought to be embraced in response to God's grace, not to guarantee it.

The Bible is a tremendous source of inspiration. Written by scores of men of faith, it is a supreme book of faith, designed to foster and promote faith. I have heard it called God's "love letter" to his people. I don't know how long it has been since you received a love letter. Before Carolyn and I were married, she lived in London for twelve months. I used to race to the mailbox every day to check for those red-and-blue bordered aerograms that I knew would be from her. Every letter was precious. I would read them ravenously, devouring every word, pondering every nuance, imagining every unwritten word. If someone had told me that all I needed to do was read a few sentences a day in order to guarantee our ongoing relationship, I would have laughed at them. How could I simply nibble at these love letters? I wanted to gorge myself on them.

It occurs to me that the Bible, like a divinely written love letter, ought to be approached with the same passion. If we are to read it, surely we should do so in response to the love that we have encountered in Jesus. To believe that we purchase the love of God by the ritualistic recitation of certain magic words is to adopt an approach quite different to that of Jesus.

Essentially, what I am talking about is called grace. This is not just the religious words you say before a meal. Grace is the term used to describe God's desire to shower you with his favor, even though you may not deserve it. It is the gift of his love. And, of course, you can't pay for a gift. All you can do is open yourself to accepting God's undeserved favor. Can you imagine how offensive it is to the giver when someone tries to pay for his gracious act?

Let me illustrate this by having you imagine that you invite me to your home for a meal. I accept. When I arrive I notice the front veranda light is on and your children are peeking excitedly through the curtains at me. I knock on the door and you all greet me in the foyer with kisses and handshakes and bring me into your warm comfortable living room. I am seated in the most comfortable chair in the house. The children crawl all over me. I am offered a glass of wine and told to kick my shoes off. We talk like old friends. Then the children head off to bed and we retire to the dining room. There is a table set for a king. The meal is brought forth and it is so magnificent that it speaks of hours of preparation. After the feast we talk for hours.

In fact, the whole the night is devoted to talking about me. You show such interest in my concerns and struggles and hopes and fears. I just feel so at home, surrounded by warmth and love and acceptance. This is grace. Then when I notice the hour and realize it's way too late to be taking up any more of your time, I jump to my feet, reach into my hip pocket for my wallet, and say, "What a lovely night. How much do I owe you for that?"

How do you feel by such offense? What an *outrage*! What you offered me was your home, your family, your time, your devotion, your love, your esteem. I can't begin to pay for that. And it is a gross insult for me to imagine that I could. This is grace—a favor that is undeserved, priceless. You can't pay for such acts of grace even if you wanted to. In God's grace he has drawn you with his loving kindness. You can't earn it. It is his free gift. What happened at the home of Simon stands to this day as a powerful and unmistakable call for repentance and devotion on the part of both the religious and irreligious. It demands a change in the lifestyles of those who have lived in immortality and carelessness and of those who have lived sanctimonious, self-righteous lives.

The fool has reframed our basic perception of forgiveness and redemption. Redemption is not earned; it is undeserved and therefore unattainable. We can only know the joy of forgiveness by throwing ourselves on the mercy of God. That kind of true repentance is only ever based on love and acceptance, not condemnation and judgment. Jesus the fool has reframed the very way we see the distinction between faithful and faithless, between devotion and ritual, between repentance and religiosity. But it's a hard lesson to learn. As I mentioned earlier, there is something within us that refuses to believe redemption can be so simple. Only a fool could believe it so.

JESUS REFRAMES OUR RELATIONSHIP WITH GOD

Luke 17:7-10

You deserve a break today.
—McDonald's advertising slogan

When I was much younger and had only recently begun this journey of faith in Jesus, I was asked by the minister at the church I was attending to speak from the pulpit and tell my story. After the service, the preacher thanked me and said, "You may never know the impact of what you had to say here tonight. But rest assured that the Lord has made use of you here. You will receive a greater crown in glory for this."

Being still at school (in my last year at high school), I was pretty tuned into rewards and merit systems and incentive schemes, so that sound of a "greater crown in glory" was reasonably appealing. So I inquired further of the evangelist about these inducements. "Oh yes," he assured me, "in heaven we will all receive a crown depending on the good works we have done in the service of our Lord."

"You mean," I pressed him, "the more you've served the Lord, the bigger and better the crown?"

He nodded very seriously. "It also applies to mansions in heaven, too, you know," he added.

Well, now he was talking. "You mean you get bigger houses in heaven depending on your life on earth?" I asked, bug-eyed.

Again, he nodded knowingly.

This system of earning celestial credit points with God seemed perfectly reasonable to me. It is, after all, the way life here on earth seems to function. We are all seeking to score points with our bosses, our teachers, our lovers, our friends. So why not with God?

As a result of that conversation, this way of thinking began to have significant impact on my faith. Whenever I performed some task that was of a "spiritual" nature (teaching Sunday school, visiting a nursing home, running a youth group), I imagined that I was racking up quite a bit of credit with God. During Jesus' time, this way of thinking and behaving was common among religious people. In fact, they believed that God was prepared to hand out bonuses here on earth *even before* we pass on to some afterlife. In other words, God doled out blessings to those he favored and curses to those he condemned. Thus, bad things happened to bad people and good things happened to good people. Of course, this equation stops making sense when bad things happen to good people. But since the basic theological presupposition is that God is never wrong, if something bad happens to a good person, then it means that the good person must be bad after all. This is the age-old dilemma.

When asked what is the most important question facing man, Albert Einstein replied, "Is the universe a friendly place?" What he meant was: can we trust that a sense of justice (friendliness) is built into our cosmos? Can the good people be assured of being looked after? It is the same dilemma faced in the old Hebrew story of Job. Here a good and righteous man is beset by one tragedy after another: his family is killed in an accident, his sheep and cattle are lost, his health fails him. Following the standard formula, his friends conclude that he mustn't have been so good and righteous after all. Remember that God sends bad things upon those who deserve it. So, if bad things are happening and God is never mistaken in his judgment, then Job must have secretly up to no good. God is cursing him, they say. The conundrum behind this very long story is that Job has not been unfaithful to his principles. He is a genuinely good man to whom bad things have happened. The story is really a tract that shows these narrow-minded theological presuppositions for what they are—hopelessly inadequate. Invariably, any formula that seeks to constrain the way God and his people interact will be found wanting, given certain individual cases.

I mentioned earlier that God will not be treated like an object who can be manipulated, depending on which buttons we press. Neither will he manipulate us. Instead, he wants to be treated as a significant other whom we encounter rather than use. And vice versa. When we serve God or others for what we can get out of it, we turn him (or them) into utilities for our personal gain. Jesus the fool radically reframed this perception in one of his encounters with his disciples, where he called into question the whole nature of religion and personal sacrifice. He bluntly suggested that if we are in this game for what we can get out of it, whether that be crowns, mansions, or individual blessings here on earth, then we have lost sight of the true value of religion and the genuine benefit of personal sacrifice. I realize that neither religion nor sacrifice are very popular ideas at the moment, but watch the fool refurbish them with a newer, more positive connotation.

Good help is hard to find

In Luke 17 Jesus tells his disciples a strangely ridiculous story about the treatment of the hired help. Jesus said, "Suppose one of you had a servant plowing or looking after sheep. Would he say to the servant when he comes in from the field, 'Come along now and sit down to eat'? Would he not rather say, 'Prepare my supper, get yourself ready and wait on me while I eat and drink; after that you may eat and drink'? Would he thank the servant because he did what he was told to do?"

The allusion is meant to be comical. Imagine, said Jesus, your servant coming in all dusty and tired from a hard day's work, and you say, "O, you look all tuckered out. Come on, stretch out on the sofa, kick those work boots off. Let me whip something up in the kitchen. Being the master, I'm not too familiar with things in there, but I can throw together a pretty tasty omelette if you like." The disciples would have been roaring with laughter. No servant would dare to expect such treatment. And no master could even think of saying anything like that.

The servant/master relationship was an enshrined institution in Palestinian culture. There were very strict guidelines regarding how servants and masters interacted. It was a secure and basic arrangement between two individuals, in which even the most caring and benevolent master would never imagine himself being in a position where he is in debt to the servant. It is always the other way round. The servant is forever in debt to his master. So, said Jesus, would a master ever thank a servant for doing what he was supposed to do? Of course not.

Well, he continued, this is how you ought to approach your relationship with God. He is our master and we are his servants. We, as servants, are forever in his debt. If we imagine that we earn extra merits or credits from him, then we are putting him in our debt and that can never be the case. He concluded: "So you also, when you have done everything you were told to do, should say, 'We are unworthy servants; we have only done our duty.'" Can you see the amazing reframe that occurs here? Often people imagine that the purpose of religion is to earn God's favor. But this reframe teaches us that living in obedience to him is done in the light of his favor, not in order to buy it.

Newer Western societies have a great deal of difficulty with Jesus' foolish words. Australia, for instance, has never really seen what a genuine servant/master relationship looks like. We are used to earning credit with our employers. We are used to overtime, paid vacation days and other considerations. I'm not saying this is necessarily a bad thing. It's just the way it is.

Britain and America have, in living memory, been familiar with this servant/master arrangement. Perhaps the best modern example I can think of is the charming American film *Driving Miss Daisy*, directed by Australian film-maker, Bruce Beresford. In this film, an aging Jewish matron and her black chauffeur, Hoke, drive together through the turbulent fifties and sixties in the southern US. Their relationship is always that of a servant/master. Even as the civil rights movement erupts around them, he is always the servant and she the master.

The charm of the film is that they both attempt to push their level of intimacy right to the very bounds of their arrangement but never beyond it. In the final scene, after he has left her employ, Hoke visits her in a convalescent hospital. She is so aged that she can't even feed herself any longer. Remember, they began their relationships in the forties when he could not vote or register in certain hotels. By now it is the seventies and he has many of the civil liberties we take for granted. But what does he do for her when he sees her in the nursing home? He feeds her. There is a sense in which he now has the dignity to perform this act of service because he chooses, rather than because he must. But nonetheless, their relationship is bound as servant/master and will be till the day they die.

As I said, we really have a lot of trouble understanding that permanent, devoted, secure contract between a master and his servant. And yet it is this very relationship that Jesus imagines us having with God. Jesus reframes the picture. God owes us nothing. We are unworthy servants. We have only done our duty.

After a servant has done his work, has he found favor with the master? Is their employer indebted to him? Is there any credit owing him? Has he earned any merit? The question is much deeper than a verbal expression of thanks. The master may well express his appreciation at the end of the day. But is the master *indebted* to his servant when orders are carried out? Jesus expects his listeners to answer, "No, of course not!"

Ray Stedman tells the tragicomical story of a missionary couple who had been missionaries for a lifetime in Africa in the nineteenth century. Having toiled long and hard at teaching, healing, caring for and liberating African tribesmen, the time of their retirement finally arrived. They booked a passage back to New York and, as fortune would have it, they found themselves sailing with the presidential entourage. Theodore Roosevelt had just completed a safari holiday shooting elephants and was returning to the States with them.

As their liner cruised passed the Statue of Liberty, the couple clambered up on deck to see whether there would be anyone awaiting them at the wharf when they arrived. It had been a long time, but they wondered whether there might be a welcoming party from their mission society with a banner or something. The dock was completely overrun by people. There were banners, brass bands, militia, governors, and other local politicians. But none of this was for the sake of the returning missionaries. The grand festivities were to welcome their president back home. The old missionary went to pieces. He wept there on the deck and cried out to his wife in the midst of the din: "We have worked our hearts out for the best years of our lives. We have done a task with eternal consequences. We have served in the name of Jesus faithfully and, when we get home, what do we get? Nothing! But this man trots off to Africa for a few weeks, shoots a couple of elephants, and is welcomed home like a hero. It's just not fair!"

They fought their way through the exultant crowd and booked into a dingy hotel in Brooklyn. He was still so upset that his wife suggested he be alone for a while to pray and contemplate. He ambled into his room, still grumbling, "We come home and what do we get? Nothing!" The some time later he emerged apparently refreshed and renewed. His face was beaming. An altogether different attitude had come over him. His wife was astounded.

"What has happened?" she asked. "You went in complaining that there was nothing here at home for us and come out looking at peace."

"That's because," he replied, "the Lord spoke and reminded me that . . . we're not home yet!"

This quaint story reminds me that if we serve the way Jesus served and live as God wants us to, we ought not do it for what rewards are in it for us. We do it out of a sense of devotion and gratitude to the one who has shown us this reason for living. It is as it was with the prostitute who anointed Jesus' feet at Simon's home. Her act of worship was not accepted by Jesus as having bought his favor. He perceived it to be a response to her having discovered his favor was already with her. This is grace. And the best religion is always enacted in response to grace.

Not getting what we deserve

We perhaps think there ought to be a celestial merit system. Jesus was keenly aware of this basic urge for extra recognition. In Matthew 20:1–16 he told another powerful story about service and reward that concerned the owner of a vineyard. The man had tended a huge crop of grapes and was ready to harvest them. He had waited until the very end of the season to ensure the plumpest and most succulent grapes and, when he felt it was time to bring them in, he had to do it quickly. So he went down to the marketplace where the laborers wait for work and contracted the biggest and strongest workmen to come and bring in the crop. They contracted to work for a denarius for the day's labor. The deal struck, he set them to work.

At about nine in the morning, he began to wonder whether the men he had hired would be able to manage the job in a day, so he went back to the marketplace to contract some more workers. But instead of contracting them, he just offered them the rest of the day's work at a reasonable price. By midday, the workers were flagging and the boss was panicking, so he raced back to the marketplace. More workers were brought in with the offer of reasonable pay. At three in the afternoon, he roped in some more workers. And at five in the afternoon he returned to scrape up the dregs, whatever good-for-nothing layabouts he could find, to finally finish off the harvest.

Well, when the work was done, the workers lined up for payment. Those who had helped polish off the job in the cool of the early evening, working only an hour of the day, received one denarius. Can you imagine how the ones who had labored all day through the heat were feeling? If the boss was paying one denarius an hour, that added up to twelve denarii for them. Hey, their ship has finally come in! But when they stepped up to the cashier's table, they were also paid one denarius. And they were furious. They complained to the boss and in Jesus' story the boss replied: "Friend, I am not being unfair to you. Didn't you agree to work for a denarius? Take your pay and go. I want to give the man who was hired last the same as you. Don't I have the right to do what I want with my own money? Or are you envious because I am generous?"

I always felt that this parable seemed a little unfair. I couldn't blame those workers for feeling that they had been treated unjustly after they had worked so hard. But then I learned something about the symbolism employed in the Bible. The coin, the denarius, is the symbol of our redemption, our salvation, eternal life. What is our salvation in Christ? Is it a gift or is it payment for services rendered? The way Jesus sees it, redemption is always a gift. So how can you complain about a gift?

Carolyn and I have three daughters. Now imagine at Christmas time, we decide to get them all the same gifts. Suppose we decide to buy them all iPods. So on Christmas morning, we give one to each of them. They are all three years apart in age. Can you see Courtney the eldest, saying, "Oh Dad, thanks for the iPod, but since I am several years older than Kendall, and six years older than Field-ing, I think that if you're going to give one iPod to the youngest, you should give two iPods to the middle daughter and three iPods to me!" Now that might be the case if Christmas gifts were in fact payment for length and service as my daughter, but they are not. They are gifts. So is salvation. The denarius paid to the workers who toiled for an hour is a gift rather than payment.

And here is the key to Christian religion. The goal of the Christian religion is not to earn salvation. Did you get that? We are not about earning redemption. Jesus' reframe says that salvation is a free gift. Call out in faith and receive it. For the Christian, religion is a life lived in service to the one who made that salvation known to him or her: Jesus of Nazareth. If we could earn redemption, then we would be putting the master in our debt. He would owe us. And as Jesus pointed out, that is never the case.

In the haunting book of Job in the Old Testament, Job experiences unspeakable suffering, including the death of his family and the loss of all his property. And yet he won't blame God for not blessing him enough. At one point he reminisces about the days when he was the most blessed of all people,

> Oh, that I were as in the months of old, as in the days when God watched over me; when his lamp shone over my head, and by his light I walked through darkness; when I was in my prime, when the friendship of God was upon my tent; when the Almighty was still with me, when my children were around me; when my steps were washed with milk, and the rock poured out for me streams of oil! When I went out to the gate of the city, when I took my seat in the square, the young men saw me and withdrew, and the aged rose up and stood . . . (Job 29:2–8)

In these days he must have felt untouchable. It was during this period of his life that he was regaled for his good works for the poor: "When the ear heard, it commended me, and when the eye saw, it approved; because I delivered the poor who cried, and the orphan who had no helper" (Job 29:11–12). It might have been easy for Job to imagine that his great reputation entitled him to certain rewards from God. But even when everything was gone, Job continued to remember that God was not his debtor.

I was speaking at a meeting once when a middle-aged man came up to me and struck up a conversation about religion. He had become a Christian, but had only recently made that commitment. He assured me that he had lived such a depraved, self-seeking existence prior to devoting himself to Christ that he felt quite ashamed of himself. I could see from his tired, lined face that he probably had burned the candle at both ends. He told me he had alienated his wife and children and most of his friends before becoming a committed Christian. Nevertheless, there was a great sense of hope and peace in his eyes. But there was one thing that bothered him.

"I have lived my life with little or no regard for anyone but myself," he said sadly, "while others have spent their entire lives following Jesus. But if my life ends tonight, I receive the same reward as they do. Redemption applies to us all equally."

I nodded. "So what's the problem with that?"

"It seems so unfair," he replied. "It just seems so unfair."

"I want you to know something," I said. "It seems unfair because God is not fair."

Now this was the last thing he expected to hear from a minister of religion and his eyes snapped open. "What do you mean? God is not fair?"

"He's not the least bit fair," I went on, "because if we got what we deserved, none of us would find salvation."

This is one of the fundamentals of the Christian faith: only when we admit that we don't deserve his mercy and call out to God in the midst of our need do we find God. In 1748 the 4th Earl of Chesterfield, a distinguished British statesman and man of letters, articulated the sensible way to view things when he said,

> Deserve a great deal, and you shall have a great deal; deserve little, and
> you shall have but a little; and be good for nothing at all, and I assure
> you, you shall have nothing at all.[13]

In other words, you get what you deserve. Chesterfield might have been a very fair-minded man, but he sees things very differently than does God. For God, it's only when we realize that we are all "good for nothing" in an eternal sense that we are able to experience the rewards he has in store for us. Maybe this is why Jesus said that it was easier for a camel to pass through the eye of a needle than for a rich man to inherit eternal life.

Where love and justice intersect

A story I read in the historical pages of the evening paper caught my eye a few years ago. It concerned the great leader of the unification of the Afghani tribes many years ago, Ahmed Shah. For centuries, the tribes of what we now call Afghanistan waged a bloody war between themselves in a hopeless, destructive series of vendettas. Finally, prompted by the fear of extinction, many of the elders of the tribes gathered to unite their people into one tribal federation and into Afghanistan. After prolonged discussion in which they could not agree on a king, the peace talks looked like they were breaking down when one of the oldest elders rose to his feet and demanded their attention. "There is only one man who could unite our tribes," he said authoritatively, "and we all know it is none of us."

They all fell silent and bowed their heads, realizing the truth of his words. There was only one man. His name was Ahmed Shah. He had left the region many years before, so disgusted was he with the bloodshed of his own people. He was said to be as strong as an ox. Word was quickly sent to him beyond the Hindu Kush offering him the position of ruler of united Afghanistan.

Ahmed Shah agreed on one condition: that he should have absolute authority. Only with unquestioned command could he unite the warring Afghani tribesmen. His terms were accepted and he took the people to a secret valley that he had discovered on his travels. It was a vast open plain, bordered on all sides by sheer cliff faces.

There was only one entrance to the basin through a deep ravine cut in the rock. He had kept the whereabouts of this entranceway secret for many years. Through the passage, he led his new nation into a future to which they looked with optimism and hope.

Once inside, life changed for the Afghanis. Used to fear and bloodshed, they now experienced peace and growth. Culture flourished. A new generation was born into a life of harmony filled with possibilities. The laws, though occasionally contravened, provided the framework for unity. And, of course, the most important law was that no one would dare to disclose the whereabouts of the secret passageway to any neighboring nations, lest these neighbors sneak in and undo all that they had struggled to achieve.

One day, Ahmed Shah was in his hut when his lieutenant walked in. He cleared his throat nervously. "Emir, we have a problem. We caught someone breaking your most important law."

"The most important law?" Ahmed Shah gasped in amazement. "You caught someone disclosing the entrance to our city?"

The lieutenant nodded. "Our secret is still safe. We apprehended the traitor and slaughtered the spies from the neighboring nation who were paying for the information."

"Well," continued the ruler, "make an example of him. Tie him to a column in the middle of the city square and have him beaten to death for everyone to see. We must show that no man can put his desires over that of the whole community. Do you hear me? One hundred lashes in the city square."

"Yes Emir, I was afraid you were going to say that. But, you see, it wasn't just anyone we caught. It was . . . er, it was . . ."

"Out with it man. Who was it?" thundered Ahmed Shah.

"It was your mother, Emir," the lieutenant stammered.

Well, you can see the crisis this posed for Ahmed Shah. Even though his lieutenant promised that he could release the mother and hush the whole matter up by killing the guards who had captured her, he knew this would make the situation even more tricky.

Surely word would get out sooner or later and the whole city would learn that he had let his mother off scot-free even though she had jeopardized the whole nation's security. Once it was known that the king had abdicated his responsibility to treat everyone equally, there would begin the rapid descent back into chaos.

But on the other hand, how can a man have his mother publicly executed as a matter of example? Who would want a king who was so heartless as to allow such a gruesome punishment to happen to his own mother? Such a king would have ice water in his veins and would lose the devotion of his people. It was a catch-22. How could he win? He was being forced to choose between his love for his mother and his commitment to justice. This was too much for a snap decision, so he dismissed his lieutenant, telling him he would make his own ruling first thing next morning.

When the sun finally burst over the cliff face and shed its light across the rocky plain, everyone gathered in the square and awaited Ahmed Shah's judgment. The accused was brought forth, still manacled. The lieutenant called for quiet, and absolute silence descended as they listened to their king. Ahmed Shah looked haggard and unkempt. Clearly, he had not slept all night. He spoke softly, but the gravity of his voice could be heard by all. He simply couldn't allow someone to risk the security of the whole city for personal profit, he said. The prisoner must die.

Women shrieked in shock. Men stood silently, their heads hung low. The old woman was manhandled to the center of the square and her hands were bound above her head to the column. The executioner stepped forward, his bull whip in his hand. There were pieces of bone knotted through the serpentine strand. It was a fearful implement. The mother's dress was torn from her back and the executioner began his dreadful business.

The first lash tore at her frail body, leaving a fiery welt. The second drew blood. Her legs began to buckle. She couldn't survive half a dozen of these blows. There was the continual hubbub of a community disgusted by the spectacle. Some stared at their king and shook their heads. They had never believed him to be like this. But as the third stroke was about to be felled, the king suddenly broke down.

"*Stop!*" he screamed, raising his huge hand. He could bear it no longer. He walked to his mother and untied her and carried her to his bed. Several of the less savory members of the community were already plotting their misdemeanors. They knew he could not pay the price of carrying out such justice. Emerging from his hut, he demanded that no one move. He had something to say.

"The penalty for my mother's crime was one hundred lashes. She has paid two of them. I will pay the other ninety-eight." And with that he removed his shirt, strode to the white column and gripped it until his knuckles turned white. Not a soul moved all morning as the executioner flailed the ninety-eight strokes across their king's back. When the harsh punishment was over, he dropped into the dust a bloodied pulpy mess, barely recognizable to them as their beloved master. No other man could ever have survived so brutal a beating. Only because of his exceptional strength was he able to cling to life. He wavered between living and dying for many anxious weeks before finally pulling through. And everyone knew that his supreme act of sacrifice was testimony to his refusal to choose between love and justice, but to remain faithful to both.

This story was told to the first British travelers to cross the Hindu Kush mountains many years ago. It had been repeated from generation to generation for centuries, such was its importance in the annals of Afghani lore. In fact, for many years rulers in Afghanistan were called "Shahs" after their first great king. The story may have suffered some in translation by the time I heard it in its current form, but I think its central focus—the struggle between love and justice—is so universal a theme as to ring true no matter the hearer. Ahmed Shah became a hero because he refused to compromise his commitment to either.

I think Jesus' sacrifice on the cross is another case of a man re-fusing to compromise his commitment to both love this world and exercise justice for all. We have all fallen short of perfection and are reminded of that fact every day of our lives. The story of the Good Samaritan illustrated it also. No matter how good we may be (and some of us are no doubt very good), we cannot love enough, care enough, serve enough to be truly perfect. So what can a perfect God have to do with imperfect beings like humans? Nothing! He cannot, by his very nature, be in contact with us. If God was interested only in being fair, he wouldn't bother with us at all. The man who spoke to me about God's seeming lack of justice was, in a sense, correct. But he was aware of only half the truth. God is not just concerned with justice. He also loves us and wants to forgive us our inadequacy, as the story of the two debtors reminds us. His dilemma is the same dreadful struggle as Ahmed Shah's. It is a tension between his justice in refusing contact with a sinful humanity and his overwhelming love for that same humanity.

When you consider the awful cost of God's refusal to com-promise between love and justice—that Jesus was sacrificed in our place—it almost seems impertinent to suggest that there ought to be some reward for services rendered in devotion to him. He said in effect: "The punishment for your sin is separation from God. You've endured that long enough. I'll take the other ninety-eight lashes." Why else do you think he cried out on that cross, "God, why have you forsaken me?" God had forsaken him because that is the penalty for sin and Jesus was bearing it on our behalf.

What response do you think Ahmed Shah might have received from his mother? Frankly, I don't know. But I can't imagine it was anything much less than humble gratitude. And surely this is the most appropriate response to grace: humility. The cross reminds us that we are always in debt to God. We are humble servants. We simply do our duty. The remarkable secret is that in doing our duty there is greater joy than we would ever have imagined. In doing our duty we reflect the same foolish, unfair love and justice that Jesus demonstrated!

Jesus reframes the way we see religion. Our lives ought to be our humble response to God's grace, not our arrogant attempts to orchestrate that grace. Our lives are lived in debt to a God who has creatively set his people free.

Sacrifice brings its own reward

Now having said all this, you would have to be pretty naive to believe that it is possible for religious people to get to the point where they are totally selfless in their devotion to God and others. After all, isn't it because of our innate selfishness that God allowed Jesus to bear the pain of death? How can he then expect us to become entirely selfless all of a sudden? Well, here is the great struggle between the real and ideal. Jesus reframes the ideal for us. But I think he recognizes that the real very often comes a long way short.

Psychotherapist M. Scott Peck invariably refuses to allow his clients to use the word "unselfish." He believes there is no such thing as a truly unselfish person. He says when he waters the flowers in his garden, he doesn't think, "Oh, flowers, look what I have done for you." He does it because he likes beautiful flowers in his garden. It is a selfish act. He firmly believes everything we choose to do is done with an eye toward some kind of reward, be it ever so small. Even the often selfless task of parenting is engaged in for some personal gain.

People often commend me for making the sacrifices I have made in order to become a minister of the church. Most people, even non-church attenders, recognize that in this line of work I am not going to make a whole lot of money. Our opportunities for advancement are limited. Ultimately, however, it was a selfish decision on our part to enter the ministry. Even those rigorous members of the Christian ministry—monks and nuns—who have denied themselves more than me (sex, marriage, children) know that the true path to joy is through sacrifice.

I mentioned parenthood briefly before and this is an example to which perhaps many of you will relate. There are enormous sacrifices to be made in the process of parenting. Carolyn and I recently completed a course called Systematic Training in Effective Parenting (STEP). We weren't really having big problems with our children but, since we were just making it all up as we went along, we thought we could do with a few more clues. When we got there we met a sad couple whose neighbors had recommended they do the course.

"Why did your neighbors recommend it? Had they also done the course?" we asked.

"Oh, no," came the reply, "they were just sick of hearing us screaming at our kids."

Every couple in our session of the course complained bitterly of enormous difficulties attached to being even mediocre fathers or mothers (often the most therapeutic part of these courses). But everyone there could say that the personal growth and development, the joy and pleasure that they had experienced as a result of the parenting process, far outweighed the sacrifice. Parents understand that sacrifice is the path to true joy.

There's an old Gerry Rafferty song with a line that goes, "I feel tired but I feel good/ 'Cause I did everything I said I would." It stuck with me because it rings so true. There is nothing so wholesome, so satisfying as the exhaustion associated with having completed a assigned task. The sacrifice involved in hard work leads directly to the satisfaction of achievement. So it is with religious life. It involves the embracing of pain and sacrifice. It involves making dreadfully difficult decisions. It involves the refusal to compromise extremely high ideals. But the payoff is the most remarkable sense of personal joy. The decision to follow Jesus and to serve him might at first seem like a very noble one, but in reality it can be an act of selfishness. It is a decision that can inevitably be made with our eyes on the prize. And this is the fabulous thing about God; even though he knows we are like that, he loves and accepts us anyway.

I was recently at a conference when this very issue was discussed. The speaker was urging us to adopt an approach to our religion that was based on selfless devotion to God in typical servant/master language. In question time, I asked her whether it wasn't impossible for us to make the decision to serve Christ completely selflessly.

"Yes," she answered, "it's altogether impossible."

"Then what's the point of trying?" I urged her.

"Because to do anything less than to try with all our might is to make a mockery of his grace," she answered with solemn wisdom.

It is a hard road, being obedient to Jesus without expecting reward in the ordinary sense. It is only with time that it might dawn on us that the sacrifices involved are themselves honoring to the very one we love—to serve God gives us its own pleasure.

JESUS REFRAMES OUR VIEW OF OTHERS

LUKE 12:13–21

> To be no part of any body, is to be nothing.
> —John Donne

The foolish perspective of Jesus affects not only our relationship to God, as we saw in the last chapter, but also the way we relate to other human beings. Jesus came as a peacemaker, preaching love and mercy. What does Jesus' foolish wisdom in these areas look like? You might be well surprised at how Jesus reframed one man's view of wealth, money, and relationships.

Sadly, it seems to be only at Christmas that we credit Jesus with being a peacemaker, the reconciler of humanity. We announce this babe at Bethlehem as bringing peace on earth and goodwill to all men and women. We seem to connect inseparably the image of a baby and the concept of peace. Perhaps that's because babies are such cute, innocent, peaceful things. When I read John Irving's whimsical novel, *The World According to Garp*, I come across a scene that I never really understood until I had children myself. Whenever the adult Garp argued with his wife, he would drag her off to the nursery to look at their sleeping children before the dispute escalated into a nasty screaming match. His rationale was that it is impossible to look upon sheer peacefulness of a sleeping child's face and stay angry with anyone. And I think I agree. The baby Jesus, wrapped tightly and placed in a manger, represents innocence, peace, goodwill—just as any tiny baby does.

The issue, however, is that Jesus did not remain a baby all his life. He outgrew the filthy eating-trough into which he was placed on his birth night. If Jesus brings peace, he brings it as a man, as Luci Shaw's extraordinary poem, "It Is as if Infancy Were the Whole of Incarnation," reminds us. She starts her poem by observing the ubiquity of images of baby Jesus at Christmastime:

> One time of the year
> The new-born child
> Is everywhere,
> Planted in Madonna's arms,
> Hay mows, stables,
> In palaces or farms, . . .

Then she notes:

> . . . But Jesus the Man is not to be seen;
> We are too wary these days
> Of beards and sandalled feet. . . .

She reminds us that

> (only the Man would give His life and live again for love of us).[14]

When we keep Christ in the manger we limit the impact the adult Jesus had on those he encountered. For it was as an adult that Jesus modeled for us the sweet, naive, innocent lifestyle of a man who steadfastly refused to be drawn into the conflict and divisions of his time. Not that he was oblivious to the culture of aggression that surrounded him. Time and again, Jesus was called upon to take sides, to endorse conflict, to champion one cause over another. And time and again, with a naiveté that Luci Shaw says "wielded peace like a sword," he brought reconciliation. With the ingénue of the fool, he pointed to a higher ideal, to a better way of relating to one another. In this way he was able to reframe the perceptions of those who came spoiling for a fight and send them away aware of another alternative.

Jesus and a matter of property

In Luke 12:13–21 Jesus was grabbed by a man in the midst of a crowd. He had, no doubt, chosen his moment carefully. It served his purposes pretty well to have his encounter with the rabbi Jesus in a public setting.

"Rabbi," he called out, approaching Jesus from the circle of listeners. "Rabbi, might I engage your services as a teacher of the Law? Would you assist me in obtaining my share of my father's inheritance from my brother?"

This wasn't an unusual request. In cases of legal disputes over inheritances Jewish law allowed for the arbitration of a rabbi. In fact, if one party and a rabbi could agree on the terms of the division of property, the second party was legally beholden to comply. Roman law, on the other hand, held that settlement could not be reached until both parties agreed, and disputes often lasted for many years. The Jewish approach certainly sped up the settlement process, but it also allowed for a few rabbis to pay off the mortgage on their beach house in Joppa more quickly.

To complicate matters, patrimony was usually passed on in the form of land. There was little liquid cash. No stocks or bonds, art collections or yacht club memberships. When a father died, he invariably left his sons dirt. But don't ever underestimate the value of a Jew leaving his sons part of Israel itself. Unless a man expressly stated otherwise, when he died his estate was split equally between his sons. Daughters inherited nothing, though the sons were obliged to care for their widowed mother and any unmarried sisters. Imagine the difficulties that arose in splitting a deceased father's land in equal portions. Even in today's world, inheritances can be messy. But when all else fails, an arbiter can simply order the property of the deceased sold and the proceeds split. Not in Israel. It was said that a man didn't own the land; it owned him. It would be anathema to suggest selling the estate and dividing the cash. The reasons these cases were held up for so long was because invariably brothers couldn't agree on the equitable division of land.

Those of us who live on standard suburban-sized blocks might think it is as simple as measuring a property in hectares or acres and splitting the figure in half. Not so. One half might have a water source and the other not. One half might be fertile and the other barren. One might have road access and the other not. One half might have the family home and the other not. In fact, equitably dividing the land into two perfectly equal estates was virtually impossible. There had to be a trade-off somewhere along the line. That is, unless you could get a rabbi to side with you, which brings us to our story.

The brother who sought to engage Jesus as his champion may very well have been within his legal rights to do so. There is nothing to suggest in the Gospel version that the man is seeking an inequitable arrangement. It may be that his brother was behaving unfairly. This man might have tried every possible avenue to settle the division reasonably and his approach to Jesus might have been the last-ditch effort. Irrespective, what we have is a man demanding that Jesus invoke his will upon his brother. He was co-opting Jesus to force his brother's hand. It may very well be a cry for justice, but it is a naked, brazen one at that.

Luke's Gospel, in which we find the account of this story, is full of Jesus' concern for the exercising of justice in human relationships. It never shies away from calling for the just and fair distribution of wealth and resources. In Luke's vision of Jesus there is a great concern for equality. But if this man was simply asking of Jesus assistance in securing his rightful property, it is hard to believe he would have done so by calling for a severing of the relationship with his brother. For that, in fact, is what he did. By publicly calling on a rabbi—and as popular a rabbi as Jesus at that—to constrain his brother to hand over the goods is virtually to cut off relations with him.

So what we have is not so much a cry for legitimate justice as a coarse, self-absorbed screech for one's rights at the expense of another's. And we all know what it looks like when various parties are prepared to sacrifice goodwill and peace in favor of "their rights."

In a middle-class suburb of St. Paul, Minnesota, a seventeen-year-old white separatist set alight a crudely fashioned cross in the yard of a black family and ignited a constitutional crisis. Charged according to a local St. Paul ordinance prohibiting the placing of symbols of hate, whether burning crosses, swastikas, or anything else, on public or private property, the youth faced a possible thirty days in jail. That was until he began calling for his rights. The First Amendment to the Constitution guaranteed him access to free speech, he claimed. To turn free expression of beliefs into a misdemeanor and charge him with disorderly conduct was downright un-American, he said. And he won (although the case was pursued to the Supreme Court).

I am not wanting to comment on the interpretation of the American Bill of Rights. I am simply illustrating what a naked cry for one's rights at the expense of other's looks like. The Minnesota youth had demanded justice and received it. But at what cost? And at whose expense? The terrified African-American family peeking out from behind their curtains?

This is Jesus' dilemma. A man inquires of him to see justice done. But at what cost? At whose expense will this man secure his rights and will it be worth it? Typical of Jesus' uncommon approach, these are the questions he turns on the man himself. He needs to have his problem reframed. He needs a fresh perspective.

What Jesus does is as if to say, "Look, this inheritance thing between you and your brother elicits a particular response in you, so you assume you know its meaning. But if you thought about it this other way, then you would have a different response." Jesus didn't transform the events themselves at all. He transformed their meaning in the mind of the one who was struggling over wealth.

He did so by abdicating his role as arbiter and handing it back to the man. Not unlike a judge stepping down from his bench and ushering the plaintiff into his seat, robing him, and pressing his gavel into his hand, Jesus said, "Who appointed me your arbiter, man? Here, you be your own judge." And raising his voice to the rest of the crowd, he cried, "Watch out! Be on your guard against all kinds of greed. A person's life does not consist in the abundance of his possessions" (Luke 12:15).

The statement, by design, was provocative. If a person's life is not defined by what he owns, how is it defined? If we are not defined by how we dress, what we drive, where we live, what we earn, how we furnish our homes, where we educate our children, how then are we defined? The man, no doubt, stepped back from Jesus. He began to realize that he might have engaged the wrong rabbi. But the rabbi was not going to let him disappear into the crowd so easily. He launched into a creative and cautionary tale, as if to say, "You came seeking wealth from me. Well, I will judge in your favor if you like. I will give you back your greatest asset. For there is far greater gain at stake here than getting your inheritance. And there is greater loss at stake than losing it."

And he told them a story. It is a story that begs the condemnation of its main character and, by inviting the man to condemn his character, Jesus the fool—Jesus the prophet—reframed this man's perceptions. At that moment, all the man wanted was his share of his father's legacy at any cost, right now. After Jesus' performance another possibility was to emerge. The court jester was to open the questioner's eyes to a new way forward. He was to invite him to condemn his own actions.

"There was a certain rich man who was desperately lonely. He had accumulated great wealth, but because he loved his possessions more than people, he had driven his family and friends away. He lived alone without a soul to share his riches with. And that's the way he liked it.

"Well, one particular season this man's property yielded a bumper harvest. Not that that's surprising. After all, as you know when you're wealthy, you can employ the best workers, purchase the best seed, and can even afford to irrigate your crop. So it may not be all that shocking to learn that his harvest was plentiful. But in this case, the man's harvest was fabulous beyond his dreams. Now if such a thing happened to you, what would you do?"

Jesus' question barely needed consideration. Every man in Israel would have dreamed a hundred times of the day he yielded a bumper crop. He would have rehearsed in his mind's eye how he would react, not unlike the way we might have dreamed of how we would react if we had won the lottery. And, of course, each man was different and would no doubt respond to good fortune differently, but there were certain conventions that few of them would have flouted. Two things needed to be done. In fact, they would have been done automatically and joyfully.

First, one would praise the living God for his mercy. This might at least take the form of a verbal affirmation—a heavily sighed "Thank God"—but it might more appropriately be expressed through the offering of a portion of the crop to the synagogue where some would be sacrificed, some kept for the maintenance of the ministry of the priests, and the rest given to the poor.

Second, they knew they would celebrate their good fortune with their community, their family, their friends. In other words, they would throw a party. Every Jew knew that without the connectedness of your community, you had nothing. To Jews in first-century Palestine, it was survival. In another of Jesus' stories, the father of the Prodigal Son immediately threw a community feast to welcome his son back. There was no such thing as a private affair. Your affairs were the community's affairs and the community's affairs were yours.

This is similar to the view presented so famously by John Donne, writing as Dean of St. Paul's Cathedral during the Great Plague in the early 1600s. As thousands of Londoners succumbed to the accursed disease, Donne grew weary of hearing funeral bells tolling for another victim. Writing about his feelings in the face of such seemingly endless death, he observed,

> No man is an island, entire of itself; every man is a piece of the continent, a part of the main. If a clod be washed away by the sea, Europe is the less, as well as if a promontory were, as well as if a manor of thy friend's or of thine own were: any man's death diminishes me, because I am involved in mankind, and therefore never send to know for whom the bells tolls; it tolls for thee.[15]

Every death matters. Every loss diminishes me, says Donne. This sense of connection to humankind set Donne apart and is reflected in Jesus' assumption about the self-centeredness of the rich fool in this parable.

"This man," Jesus continued, "held no feast. He attended no synagogue. He sat back and gloated in his good fortune." And with that, Jesus had said a mouthful. He had neatly sketched the most pathetic of images; a man with everything to live for, who has refused to live, who disconnected himself from life, from God, from his community. He is a contemptible and rueful character. In fact, if this were vaudeville, we would be booing him at this point.

"Of course," Jesus went on, "weighing heavily on his minds was what to do with the huge crop. Even though he was wealthy, he had never counted on a harvest this large. He didn't have barns big enough to store it all."

Now, it was common in Jesus' time for the leading men of a community to sit at a gate and to discuss at length any issue or concern that might be raised. Elders decided their course of action in community after hours of parry and thrust, to-ing and fro-ing.

Kenneth Bailey, a biblical scholar who has spent many years in the Middle East, says that there is a subtle pressure at these discussions not to introduce the information that will settle the question under discussion. The rationale seems to be, "We have a satisfying debate going here, so don't spoil it." Anyway, the point is that Middle Easterners prefer to make up their minds in a crowd, in community, after hours of discussion with their friends.

This may be so very different from the way we Westerners communicate. Essentially, we talk to each other for the sake of expediency. If there is an item on the agenda requiring a decision, we make it our goal to decide it with as little discussion as possible. In fact, we become frustrated if the talking drags on too long. Each member of the group only contributes in order to conclude the discussion. This is to our loss for, when communication is only valuable for the purposes of getting things done, the next step is to treat people the same way—as valuable only to the degree that they help us to get things done. Imagine how different it is when each member contributes only to prolong proceedings. In a sense, we communicate functionally; Middle Easterners communicate for the sake of communicating.

Of course, the degree to which this is true varies from one culture to the next. A subplot of the Spike Lee film *Do The Right Thing* follows a group of older black men sitting on a street corner ranting and raving, singing, laughing, swearing, fighting, making social comment, drinking, and generally creating community. It is as if Spike Lee gives us just a glimpse into the black Brooklyn street-corner culture to remind us that the dialogue doesn't always have to be going somewhere. There can be dialogue for the sake of dialogue. Another American filmmaker, Martin Scorsese, calls it street-corner chatter. His films are filled with it. In Jesus' day, those sitting at the gate would have been street-corner chatterers.

That the rich man in Jesus' story did not immediately give his due to God or celebrate his great fortune with his friends and family is shocking enough, but the fact that he sat alone at home deciding how to invest his wealth would have been all the more pathetic.

The man in the story did not head for the city gate. There was no street-corner chatter. There was only the silence of a lonely man.

The juxtaposition of images is remarkably creative. Jesus' audience would have been assailed by mixed signals. On the one hand, the man is to be admired for his wealth and good fortune. On the other hand, he is to be pitied for his being alone and disconnected. Jesus' listeners would not have been certain whether to regard him as a very rich man or a very poor man. And this is the brilliance of Jesus' performance.

But he continued: "And so alone he determines to hoard his wealth, to tear down the barns he has and to build bigger barns to store his fabulous crop. The investment would have secured him for life. There was no suggestion that he give some to the poor or the priest or his family—for who does not have a family?—or his friends or as a reward to his workmen. He determined to invest it all in his own future. And in his dreams, he stood in the long shadows of his new barns and stared with admiration at them as symbols of his achievement and prestige. He decided to take life easy, to eat, drink, and be merry."

Mind you, this was in itself no crime. Every man would have imagined the day when he could say those very things to himself. The crime, rather, is that he had determined to do all these things alone. To eat alone, to drink alone, to be merry alone is to waste the effort as far as Jesus' audience was concerned. The story had run its course by now. The listeners were convinced that, despite his great financial wealth, this man was poverty-stricken beyond belief. Then the story took a new turn as God's voice thundered onto the scene.

"But God said to him," Jesus said, his voice perhaps deepened by the gravity of his statement, "You fool! This very night your life will be demanded from you. Then who will get what you have prepared for yourself?"

Deliberately, Jesus may have paused. This was the crux. Who will get what you have prepared for yourself? The answer, as they all knew, was that no one would get it. There were no friends left. There was no family. No sons by his side. No daughters to care for him on his deathbed. No fellow Elders mourning at the gate. He had lived alone and would die alone. And in Jewish thinking, there was no greater curse than to die alone. If there was such a concept as immortality for the Jews, it was in remembrance; to be remembered, to live on in the memories of those whose lives you had touched was to achieve eternal life.

I heard an American rabbi telling the story of his grandfather, a Ukrainian potato farmer, who had been a man of scrupulous honesty and integrity in a society that fostered deceit and selfishness. At the end of his life, everyone asked what the use was of him being so honest. Others had profited during their lives by their underhandedness and made a better life for their families than he had by remaining unshakable in his honor. He died as poor a potato farmer as he began.

"But," said the rabbi telling the story, "after all the other potato farmers in the Ukraine were long forgotten, the community continued to remember and recall my grandfather and his grand integrity. Why, I am even celebrating his honor now by telling you."

And so our man in Jesus' story died as forgotten and unremarkable as the other potato farmers in that Ukraine community. In fact, if he were to be remembered at all it would be for his folly, for his self-centeredness, for his loneliness. If he did live on it would be only as a reminder to others of what a wasted and destitute life looks like. Jesus concluded his tale by confirming once and for all that this man was not the least bit rich. He was poor, tragic, alone.

And then Jesus turned to the man who first invited this exchange, the one seeking his share of his father's inheritance, who by now must have been sorry he brought the topic up in the first place. Jesus said, perhaps quietly but deliberately: "This is how it will be for anyone who stores up things for himself, but forgets what things really make you rich in this world." He might as well have said: "You be the judge. If you condemn this man, you condemn yourself, just like David was forced to condemn himself. And in the light of that condemnation do you still imagine the greatest asset you have available to you is your father's legacy? Do you not see now that your greatest wealth lies in your relationship with your brother? Would you still squander that relationship for half the land your father left you? If so, go right ahead. But you will be all the more poorer for having done so."

Reconciliation and companionship

Jesus steadfastly refuses to be drawn as an agent of division or separation. He is about bringing people together. His is a mission of reconciliation and, while he realizes that the radical lifestyle to which he calls his followers may sometimes result in division, he is most concerned about the healing of brokenness and the promotion of good will. And these concerns he shares with God.

God is primarily committed to the process of putting people together. In fact, if you read the first few chapters of Genesis, in the story of God's creativity in this world you will find an interesting pattern emerging. Time and again, in the created order of things, God separates. He separates light and darkness. He separates the sky from the earth. He separates the land from the sea. He separates the creatures of the earth from the creatures of the ocean from the creatures of the air. But when it comes to human beings, what does he do? He puts them together. In Genesis 2:18 God says, "It is not good for man to be alone." He creates human beings to be together.

This is what the great illustration of marriage is all about. Two people commit themselves to become one, to be put together. We often make the mistake of thinking that married couples become "one" on their wedding day, as if the magical words of the minister or the mystical experience of the marriage bed constitute this process. They do not. They only inaugurate the process. The process of being one is just that—a process. A couple will spend the rest of their lives working towards it. But they are only a microcosm of that to which all human beings are called. This togetherness is best summed up by the term "companionship." We are called by God to be companions, which comes from the Latin *cum panis* ("with bread"). We are here to share bread with one another, to be at one.

There are many names for this sharing: utopia, community, the kingdom of God. It is this sharing to which Jesus calls us. Only in this context can we ever be considered wealthy. Richness is available only to the degree that we are prepared to be put together with one another. It is the highest of callings, the most difficult of missions.

Churches, if they are gatherings of those committed to the causes of Jesus, ought to be the most "put together" places of all. Church are groups of people committed to the mission of companionship, the sharing of bread, the creation of community. The parable of the rich fool, as it is called, is a cautionary tale reminding us that poverty results from self-interest and greed. If we feel called to follow Jesus, we must necessarily feel called to the enormous task of overcoming such self-interest and greed and embracing acceptance and love and generosity.

It has been said that the church—and remember that the word "church" didn't originally mean a big ecclesiastical organization—is God's experimental garden in the world. It is God's model farm. The word "church" simply means "the called ones." It is used in the New Testament to refer to those people who believe they are called to follow in the way of Jesus. These people are to model, to experiment with a different way of living together that all might share in their companionship.

When the east coast of Australia was first settled by Europeans in 1788 it was discovered that, as beautiful as Sydney Harbour might be, the whole Sydney area was in fact a sandstone shelf, great for building cities, but terrible for producing crops. So the new colony nearly starved to death. They were forced to rely on supply ships from home to feed the burgeoning new nation. Then in 1792 a convict named James Ruse asked the governor for a grant of land north-west of the westernmost part of the colony at Parramatta. He was to hack out of the virgin bush and scrub land a viable farm. Until this time, the only farms were really riverfront estates clinging precariously to the Parramatta River. James Ruse's grand experiment was seen as a barometer to the continued survival of Sydney. The Great Dividing Range had not yet been crossed and the vast tracts of rolling pasture not yet discovered. It was James Ruse or bust. In fact, Ruse called his property Experiment Farm, rather than naming it after his home town in Britain like most others did. In a sense, the whole colony held its breath and awaited the outcome. This was an experiment that could not afford to fail.

After a couple of dismal attempts, the farm finally produced a useful harvest. Experiment Farm was renamed Model Farm, for that is what it had become—a model for others to follow. The mountains were eventually crossed and the fertile inland of New South Wales changed the situation altogether. Model Farm served as an inspiration to others that hard work, vision, and commitment can save the day.

This is the mandate of the church of Jesus—to be an Experiment Farm. If only the world were holding its breath awaiting the outcome. Sadly, the world has given up on the church as a failed experiment. But that need not be the end of the story. As German theologian Jurgen Moltmann says, the church can be a way of living together that affirms that no one is alone with their problems: that no one has to conceal their disabilities; that there are not some who have all the say and others who have nothing to say; that neither the elderly nor the very young are isolated; that no one can dismiss another even when there is unpleasant disagreement. In such a place, every member would be rich indeed.

A true church should transcend every barrier imposed by family, class, or culture. The community of believers should not be about winning people like themselves to themselves. It should be about sharing the good news that Jesus first shattered the barriers that divide the human race and then created a new community. While some might consider this new people of God a sociological impossibility for people—regardless of their culture, language, race, or custom—to develop this oneness, it is an impossibility that nevertheless has become possible. Do you want to know what things really make one rich? It is not your barns or your crops, it is your brothers and your sisters.

Jesus was not alone in teaching this view. The apostle Paul was equally committed to the development of this new community. Typically, he was more blunt and to the point than Jesus and somewhat less creative. His concern was not to play the court fool as Jesus had, but to distill the insights of Christ and to hit his listeners right between the eyes. His simplest maxim for community life is found in Romans 5:7: "Accept one another then, just as Christ has accepted you, in order to bring praise to God."

When Paul wrote these words, he had in mind the Christian church at Rome that consisted of both Jews and Gentiles. The Jewish Christians were in the minority and yet were esteeming themselves as true believers. They viewed Gentile believers as second-rate Christians. In our time conflict between Jewish and Gentile Christians is certainly not a problem, but conflict between other varieties of Christians is all too common.

Companionship and reconciliation and the spirit of our age

We have become a culture of individualists, all calling for our rights at the expense of others. The result is that our societies have become inevitably fractured. Whenever a strong individualism is not balanced by a commitment to companionship then isolation and fragmentation become the order of the day. The real disabilities in our culture, as in Christ's, are human isolation and a sense of rejection from one's environment. The reality is that we can never be completely whole in and of ourselves. We need others to make our lives complete. Did you hear that? We need each other. There is a point beyond which our sense of self-determination becomes inaccurate, arrogant, and increasingly self-defeating. Here we have the point of the parable of the rich fool. We are inevitably social creatures who desperately need each other not merely for sustenance or for company but for any meaning to our lives whatsoever.

I recently heard of an experiment—a pretty cruel one, actually—in which individual horses were kept in paddocks away from roadways or rivers in order to minimize the likelihood of them ever seeing another living creature. They were fed and watered under cover of darkness so that the horses never laid eyes on those caring for them. All the fresh water, fresh food, shelter, fresh air and exercise they needed were available to them. And yet they never encountered any animals or humans. And in each and every case, the horses became desperately ill, almost to the point of death. They were literally dying of loneliness.

It is not true that all we need to exist is fresh food, fresh air and fresh water. We need significant human contact. We need each other. But it should be pointed out that when Paul told the Romans to accept one another, he anticipated something more than mere tolerance. He anticipated an acceptance that transcended usual human boundaries. Paul's ideal was contrary to Aristotle's old principle for human community, "Birds of a feather flock together." Aristotle says that we feel confirmed by people who think like us, who act like us, who desire similar things in similar ways. People are affirmed by those who are the same as them. Conversely, we feel insecure around those who are quite different from us in fundamental ways, whose ambitions, ideals, priorities, and desires differ from ours. Therefore, we enjoy those who are like us and shun those who are different. It is simply a social form of self-justification.

Yet Paul's message was to accept one another "as Christ has accepted you." It is this extraordinary dynamic that makes Christian community capable of achieving utopia. It is this dynamic that makes Christian community the "new way of living." Only such an orientation that recognizes Christ's acceptance of us can move a disparate bunch of believers towards genuine oneness. An understanding of our acceptance by Jesus frees us to forget about the need for self-confirmation because we are no longer made to feel insecure by others. We can mutually accept one another because Christ has accepted us. And in that knowledge we are confident enough to accept, recognize, and confirm others, even those who are different from ourselves. We stop crying for our rights.

In this type of community, we recognize our greatest riches lie in our relationships, especially in those with people who differ from us. In this type of community we would come together not to confirm ourselves but to offer acceptance and love even to the most unlovely. As a result, real communities, if they want to remain such, are always reaching to extend themselves. The burden of proof falls on exclusivity. True communities do not ask, "How can we justify taking this person in?" Rather, the question becomes, "Is it at all justifiable to keep this person out?"

Jesus' story about the rich fool highlights this fact. There are greater riches in this world than your money, your property, your rights, your prestige. They are companionship, the sharing of bread, being put together with others, community. These things are valuable beyond our comprehension. The squabbling over land at the expense of your relationship with your brother is the most contemptible act as far as Jesus was concerned. And, be sure, we must not let the agrarian imagery trick us up here. We, in our urban-based societies, are as likely to lose sight of the really important things in life as anyone.

I had a friend who was working for a large and successful multinational corporation and was moving his way very quickly up the corporate ladder. He was married and had two little girls, both preschoolers. As his friend, I became put out when he seemed to have less and less time for me. And when he did find the time, he was always rushed, tired, and preoccupied. I raised this with his wife one day and she shared similar frustration. She was particularly concerned that he never seemed to see their children. He left for work while they were still sleeping and often returned long after they had been tucked back in bed.

One afternoon, Carolyn and I were visiting them when he launched into a great tirade about the pressure he was currently facing at the office. He went to considerable lengths to explain that someone above him on the ladder had retired and there had been a shuffle upwards throughout the company. This had meant a slight promotion for him. We told him we were very happy for him. But what was creating the stress?

Well, he said, whenever anyone was promoted, one of the benefits, aside from an increase in salary, was a parking space closer to the main entrance of the buildings. Now it seemed that someone below him in the pecking order had taken his parking spot. He had spent a harrowing week negotiating the interloper out of this parking space. There had been much interdepartmental politicking going on until finally the insubordinate had been deposited back down to his rightful spot. This return to order had required quite a few extra hours at the office. My friend explained to us that we had no idea how much stress had been associated with this venture.

"Well," I asked, "does it really matter if your car is 103 yards away from the front door rather than 100? I mean is that important?"

"You don't understand," he snapped back. "It's my right. I'm entitled to that space. After all, if these guys find out I'm a pushover in the parking lot, they'll treat me like a pushover in the boardroom. My integrity is at stake."

What he meant was his integrity as a high-powered business executive was at stake, not necessarily his integrity as a human being.

And what he meant was that asserting his rights in the parking lot was worth alienating several departmental heads and assorted corporate heavy-hitters. It was worth spending time fighting that could otherwise have been spent with his family. To me, a parking spot did not seem worth all that. But then I am not and have never been employed by a large competitive organization (unless you count the church). The culture in which my friend was immersed had conditioned him to believe that this issue really was worth such a cost. When you think like that, it is not such a long time before you begin to treat people as objects who either contribute to you reaching your goals or obstruct you from doing so.

No doubt the man who confronted Jesus about his inheritance had been seduced into thinking this way, too. This just reinforces our observation that Jesus' parable here was radical in its call to his listeners to see another way of living, to see the great value in relationships as opposed to rights, property, or position.

It reminds me of the story of a young boy who had been pushed all his life to achieve, to be number one. He was told throughout high school that he was the most important person in the world, that he should let no one stand in the way of his goals. He was pushed to earn the best grades at his school. He applied to medical school and was the top entering student. After completing his first year, his parents gave him a trip to Japan as a reward. In Japan he encountered a Buddhist monk who taught him the secrets of selflessness and inner peace. Well, after a life of competition and achievement, he was ripe for this kind of teaching. He wrote to his parents that he would not be returning to medical school. He was going to become a Buddhist monk.

Six months later, he wrote again to his parents. In his letter he said, "I know you were bitterly disappointed with me for not returning and continuing my studies, but if only you knew how happy I am here at the temple. I have found an inner solitude and peace that has delivered me from self-centeredness. I have discovered the foolishness of human achievement at any cost. Oh, by the way, I am studying hard and was placed second best disciple in the order. I know with a little more work next year I can make number one."

It is hard to remember that people are more important than property, power, programs, or prestige. As a minister, this is a lesson I need to be reminded of regularly. I recently had a young family arrive at our church and tell us they wanted to be involved. We were thrilled to have them, as anyone would be, and welcomed them with open arms. The husband told me that he was a signwriter and that he specialized in rustic, wood-carved signs. He asked whether we would like one outside our church. Thinking it would lift our rather drab-looking building, I was delighted and told him so. He told me it would be ready in a few weeks. A few days later his wife walked out on him. At that moment his life fell apart.

This impending marriage crisis was what had initially motivated them to reach out to our church, and we rallied to their side, counseled them both extensively and sought to bring about a reconciliation. Unfortunately, things looked more and more bleak as time went by. Every day I dropped around to see him at his home, I noticed the beautiful half-finished sign in his garage. It looked great. But since I was there to support him in his loneliness I usually avoided even mentioning it. As more time went by, however, I found myself more concerned to see how the sign was progressing than to see how he was progressing. At meetings of the pastoral staff, I would often raise the question of how he was doing in the hope of getting our hands on the sign rather than helping him. Subtly and yet powerfully, I was making the shift from genuine concern for people to a single-minded concern for my property.

Your brother is a greater asset than your land, Jesus cries. And adherence to this principle takes considerable commitment in the face of the great pressure to conform to a generally self-centered culture. Malcolm X, the civil rights leader of the 1960s, voiced the spirit of our age when he said,

I believe in the brotherhood of man, all men, but I don't believe in brotherhood with anybody who doesn't want brotherhood with me. I believe in treating people right, but I'm not going to waste my time trying to treat somebody right who doesn't know how to return the treatment.[16]

One might empathize with Malcolm, particularly in light of his treatment by white society at that time. But too many people voice this same attitude today. It is played out between nations and between individuals everywhere.

A tale of true companionship

In this regard, we might rehearse another magnificent story. This is not one of Jesus' stories, but it might as well be. It has been transposed into prose from a poem by Kenneth Bailey in his book *Through Peasant Eyes*.[17]

There once were two brothers in Palestine, one of whom was very wealthy, the other desperately poor. The rich brother was alone for he had no children, while the poor brother had many sons and daughters. It seemed to others that this was dreadfully inequitable, for the rich brother had no one to share his wealth with and the poor brother had great difficulty feeding his large family. But in spite of this disparity, they were as close as brothers could be.

One day, their father called them together. He explained that he was very ill and did not expect to last until evening. He wanted them to be clear about the fact that they were to divide their inheritance equally. In fact, he told them, he had set a post in the center of his property to mark the division. It was his desire that there be no squabbles after he had gone. The post, he thought, would maintain the unity between his sons that he had so admired. Sure enough, that day he passed quietly from this world. The two brothers buried him respectfully before nightfall, as custom dictated.

That night, as the rich brother lay in bed, he could not sleep. "What my father did was quite unfair," he mused. "I have more wealth than I know what to do with, while my brother works like a dog just to make ends meet. His children starve while I eat my fill. I know what I'll do. I'll give my brother a gift of the larger portion of the inheritance." But he suspected that his brother was too proud to accept such a gift, so he determined to get up early, before sunrise, and move the post to ensure his brother the lion's share of the legacy.

That night, the poor brother tossed restlessly on his bed. "What my father did was quite unfair," he thought. "I am surrounded by the love of my children, while my brother continually faces the shame of having no heirs to carry on his name, no daughters to care for him in his old age. To compensate him for his poverty, I will make him a gift of the greater share of our father's inheritance." But he knew that his wealthy brother would never accept a gift like that from his poorer brother, so he set himself to rise early, while it was still dark, and move the post in order to ensure that his brother received the lion's share of the inheritance.

The next morning, while the air was crisp and the sky still black, when not a sound could be heard, two brothers met at the post and embraced each other with tears of love. It was said that on that site the city of Jerusalem was built.

JESUS REFRAMES OUR ATTITUDE TO THE POOR

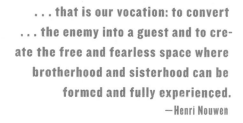

LUKE 16:1-13

> . . . that is our vocation: to convert
> . . . the enemy into a guest and to cre-
> ate the free and fearless space where
> brotherhood and sisterhood can be
> formed and fully experienced.
> —Henri Nouwen

What do you think about when you see the poor? Whether it's a panhandler on a city street corner or a picture of a starving child from Africa, do you see despair or laziness? Do you react with compassion or disinterest? Do you cry out to God or blame him?

In Jesus' time, the poor were seen as the example of what happens to us if God is *not* with us. In John 9 Jesus' disciples point out a man who had been blind since birth. With such a disability the man would have been poor indeed, since he couldn't work and there was no social security system for people like him. The disciples' question to Jesus reveals how the poor were seen at that time: "Rabbi, who sinned, this man or his parents, that he was born blind?" (John 9:2). They naturally assumed that the poor (or their parents) must have sinned to be in such a sorry state. But Jesus the fool reframes the way we see the poor, and God and ourselves. To the disciples' question he insists, "Neither this man nor his parents sinned." And then he says rather cryptically, "He was born blind so that God's works might be revealed in him," before swiftly healing him (John 9:3–7). How do we see the "works of God" in the plight of the poor? Jesus has another foolish story for us to answer that question.

The dishonest manager

In Luke 16:1–9 Jesus tells one of his most troubling stories. It is troubling because in it he dares to create his most opportunistic and dishonest character, a man who has much to teach us by his shrewd self-interest and initiative. Only a fool would have the nerve to commend so despicable an individual. Today he is known as the dishonest manager.

In this story a wealthy landlord owns large tracts of property, rented by various tenants who work the land and pay him at harvest time in kind, rather than in cash. Managing these affairs is time-consuming and the landlord installs a manager or realtor to negotiate the rents for each tenant and collect the bulky goods offered in payment. From the way the story unfolds it becomes obvious that the landlord must be a fabulously wealthy man. So large is his estate that he entrusts it totally to his manager and has little to do with its day-to-day administration.

It is this lack of close scrutiny that allows the manager enough freedom to skim a bit of profit for himself off the top of each renter's bill. In every likelihood, each tenant had to agree to a fixed amount of produce for the yearly rent. But the manager was making extra in "under the table" transactions that were never reflected in the signed bills. This was in addition to the commission he was paid by the landlord on each transaction. The dishonest manager was ripping off both his boss and his clients. Nice work if you can get it, I suppose. The steward barely has to lift a finger. The wealthy man owns the property. The tenants work the property. And the manager profits from both. Of course neither the landlord nor the tenants knew about it. The tenants would have thought that the landlord was charging premium rents, not knowing part of it was never getting past the manager.

In Jesus' telling of this story, we enter the drama just as the landlord gets wind of his manager's duplicity. Having heard that he is being taking advantage of, and knowing that his tenants are suffering under exorbitant rents to line the manager's pockets, he calls his agent to account for his dishonesty. The manager knows that the game is up and has no answer. He realizes there is no way he can conceal his fudging of the books. He is on the verge of being fired from the best job he has ever had.

Up to this point Jesus' working-class listeners wouldn't have seen anything unusual in all of this. They knew well what it was like to be ripped off by their landlords' managers and by the Romans' tax-collectors, all of whom often added ridiculous commissions and made capricious demands for extra payments. When the obviously noble landlord addresses the situation by planning to fire his agent, it would have seemed like sweet justice. The landlord would have been justified in suing his manager and throwing him in prison until he could reimburse him for his losses. His decision to only fire him is indication of his extraordinary grace and mercy. The wealthy landlord is the good guy and the dishonest manager is the bad guy. Jesus' listeners would have guessed that the moral of this story is probably something like, "Beware, your sins shall find you out." Simple. But what happens next is the work of a master-storyteller. It is the Fool at his most disarming.

The quality of mercy

Firstly, Jesus lets his listeners in on just how desperate the manager's situation is. He has the manager fretting over the possibility of taking up manual labor, or worse, begging, just to survive!

What will I do, now that my master is taking the position away from me?
I am not strong enough to dig, and I am ashamed to beg. (Luke 16:3)

How his listeners would have laughed. The bad guy gets his comeuppance. It was outrageous for an educated man in authority to even consider digging. This manager rejects the idea, not because it is beneath him, but because he is too physically weak to pull it off. More peals of laughter would have rippled through the crowd. A dishonest man dismissed for incompetence was virtually unemployable. Surely God was not on the side of this scoundrel. Jesus has set up a situation where his audience would have assumed that the manager was an example of what *not* to do. But the Fool is about to reframe the entire scenario by inventing a masterful escape, one that would have left his audience astonished. By the time it is over the manager will become an example of exactly what we *are* to do as we encounter the Kingdom of God!

Knowing that the only thing he has going for him is that no one yet knows he has been fired, the manager concocts a brilliant and dastardly strategy. Remember that his landlord is a man of considerable patience. He has already refrained from throwing his employee in prison, though he would be justified in doing so. The manager decides to risk everything on the quality of mercy he has already received from his boss. If he blows it, he will certainly be thrown in jail. If he succeeds, however, he will be a hero in his community and will have gained friends for himself, people who could likely help him in the future.

Working quickly, before news of his dismissal gets out, the manager summons all the tenants to individual meetings, dealing with them one by one to ensure they don't have time to talk to each other, nor to ask too many questions. Not knowing of his dilemma, they would have assumed he was acting on behalf of their landlord. And this is exactly what he wants them to assume. Most renters trusted their landlords. Kenneth Bailey quotes Asher Feldman's commentary on the rabbinical parables of the time, as saying, "Personal relations [between landlords and renters] were often friendly—sometimes quite intimate."[18]

A landlord as merciful as the one in Jesus' story would have been much loved by his tenants. Although they would have been curious about the timing of the meeting, since it wasn't harvest time and the outstanding bills wouldn't have been due yet, they would have attended a meeting with his manager expectantly, not suspiciously.

"How much do you owe my master?" he asks each renter, clearly implying he was still in the landlord's employ. As the unsuspecting renters explain the details of their bill—100 jugs of olive oil, 100 containers of wheat—the manager scratches his beard and nods sympathetically. What he does next is cunning in the extreme. Letting the tenants think the landlord has approved of his action, he slashes their rent by up to 50 percent, telling them to rewrite the bill in their own hand. Further, he allows them to assume that he, the manager, had a hand in this extraordinary act of generosity. To do so, he needn't actually have said anything. The bills are not due. These sudden reductions have come totally out of the blue. Or, of course, he might have even let it slip, "Yeah, I talked the old man into it. I know how tough the weather's been lately. You guys can do with a break." The tenancy laws at that time allowed for a reduction in rent if a tree died, or blight spread across the a field, or a spring dried up. The manager milked this for all it was worth. Kenneth Bailey describes this deceit charmingly,

> The [manager] thus achieves the position of a factory foreman who has arranged a generous Christmas bonus for all the workers. The bonus itself is from the owners. But the foreman is praised for having talked the owners into granting it.[19]

Imagine the response from the community! An impromptu celebration would have resulted. There would have been dancing in the streets. Glasses would have been raised in toasts to their noble landlord who had generously relieved them of up to half their rent. And while these raucous celebrations began the dishonest manager would have gathered up the newly minted tenancy agreements and delivered them to his unsuspecting master.

The wealthy landlord would have immediately known that he had only two options. First, he could fire the manager, hand him over to the authorities and go back to his tenants and explain that it was all an awful hoax and the rent reductions were null and void. But he knew that to do so would forever alter the quality of his relationship with his renters. Their relief would turn to anger and he would be cursed for his tight-fistedness. And we know this was a good man, with a generous heart, something the manager was banking on.

His second option was to keep silent, to accept the community's praise and to let the manager bask in his reflected glory as having engineered this amazing act of generosity and now having all the tenants in his debt. Imagine the landowner smiling and waving to his exultant workers, while whispering through gritted teeth to his manager beside him, "You *are* a cunning old fox, aren't you?" The landlord had been cleverly tricked by the quality of his own mercy. The duplicitous manager has turned the tables. By a second act of dishonesty he saves his own neck, while enhancing his boss's reputation and delivering financial relief to the community. Jesus' audience falls silent. They nod approvingly. That wasn't what they had expected, but even they had to admire the manager's knack for self-preservation.

Making friends using filthy lucre

This crafty real estate agent has gone from being the classic villain to becoming a highly praised example of the Kingdom of God. But how? What is it about this cheeky manager that is so commendable? His self interest? His craftiness? Well, yes and no. Jesus commends him not for his dishonesty but rather for his "wisdom" in working out which side his bread was buttered on. The wisdom of the manager is that he fully understood his situation was hopeless, but for the patience and mercy of the master. He came to a point where he knew he was at the end of his human capacities. He recognized his impotence and gambled on the landlord's grace.

This is what the Kingdom of God is like, says Jesus. It is full of dishonest, disreputable people, who have no way of earning their salvation. What marks them out is that they have realized their hopelessness and banked on the mercy and grace of God. If an ordinary, though obviously noble, man like the landlord can be won over by the cleverness of his desperate manager, how much more would our infinitely patient and gracious God be "won over" by our desperate pleas for salvation?

As mentioned earlier, this was a classic rabbinical technique of the time, called the principle of "from the light to the heavy," which generally means, "how much more." Jesus uses it several times. In Luke 18 he refers to a persistent widow who badgers a judge into granting her justice. Jesus concludes that if this cranky judge can grant her request, "how much more will your Father in heaven answer your petitions." In Luke 11 a man gets bread from a neighbor in the middle of the night. If this can happen, how much more will you receive from God who wants to bless you, says Jesus.

So, if the dishonest manager is bailed out by his generous boss, how much more will God bail us out if we throw ourselves on his mercy. But in this instance, Jesus goes further by offering an extra "moral" to his ingenious story:

> And I tell you, make friends for yourselves by means of dishonest wealth so when it is gone, they may welcome you into the eternal homes. (Luke 16:9)

What? Make friends using "dishonest wealth" (or *filthy lucre* as in the older translations)? What does Jesus mean by this cryptic phrase? At first glance it might sound like he is endorsing a form of salvation by works: use your money to buy friends and then when you die you'll go to heaven. But that would contradict all that has gone before. The parable is about someone who cannot buy his way out. He's trapped. It is by the landlord's grace alone that he survives. This is clearly a parable of grace, but Jesus uses the opportunity to say something extra about how we conduct our affairs. It seems that this story says two things: firstly, we will be rescued only when we realize our hope rests entirely in God's hands; and secondly, while counting on God's grace, we are to give wealth away to those in need. Our salvation is given freely by God, but our journey toward heaven should be lined with those we have helped financially.

This is another example of the "how much more" approach. If a self-interested fellow like our manager can relieve the suffering of others, how much more can we, freely forgiven by God's grace, help those in need by acts of generosity and kindness? Jesus goes on,

> No slave can serve two masters; for a slave will either hate the one and love the other, or be devoted to the one and despise the other. You cannot serve God and wealth. (Luke 16:13)

His dramatic conclusion to this story is that when you have given your allegiance to God you become his "slave." Your gratitude for his mercy is so great that you'd do anything for him. Therefore, you are to be no longer enamored of material wealth. It should have no hold on you. You are free from its mastery, and the obvious way to demonstrate your freedom is to give your money away! This is what it is like in the Kingdom of God: the value of money has been completely reoriented. Its primary value now rests in its utility in being something to give away.

Nowhere is this more obviously demonstrated than in the lifestyle of Jesus himself. He is free from the bonds of slavery to material wealth. In Matthew 8:20 he says: "Foxes have holes, and birds of the air have nests; but the Son of Man has nowhere to lay his head." This is not just some poetic saying. He is announcing that birds and foxes are better off than him. He is a homeless, itinerant rabbi, living at the mercy of others. And yet, just shortly after saying this, we find Jesus in a boat with the disciples on the Sea of Galilee with a ferocious windstorm whipping up around them. The disciples fear for their lives, but Jesus is sleeping in the boat. Just earlier he had told them that the Son of Man has nowhere to lay his head. Here he is laying his head in a boat. The conclusion is obvious: Jesus has no home, but in his poverty he is completely free to lay his head *anywhere*.

What else is there to do with money if it has no hold on you? Why, give it away, of course. This is exactly what French philosopher/ theologian Jacques Ellul said about the de-sacralizing of filthy lucre. While many Christians seem to think of money as a neutral thing, merely a tool that we can use for either good or ill, Ellul believed it to be much more. Far from being neutral, he said, money is a powerful agent that sets itself against the Kingdom of God. While the Kingdom is about grace, money is about everything but. It has an ungodly, re-ligious power that directs us away from grace. It is all about assessing worth, buying and selling, and economies of scale. Grace is about us receiving what we're *not* due and about being valued above our worth.

Ellul believed that followers of Jesus needed to take his advice about money in Luke 16 and give it away. In fact, by giving it away, by "gracing" money this way, we break its spiritual power in our lives. In his book, *Money and Power*, Ellul called this de-sacralizing of money *profanation*. He said, "To profane money, like all other powers, is to take away its sacred character."[20] And he went on to say,

> This profanation, then, means uprooting the sacred character, destroy-ing the element of power. We must bring money back to its simple role as a material instrument. When money is no more than an object, when it has lost its seductiveness, its supreme value, its superhuman splendor, then we can use it like any other of our belongings, like any machine. Of course, even if this relieves our fears, we must al-ways be vigilant and very attentive because the power is never totally

eliminated. Now this profanation is first of all the result of a spiritual battle, but this must be translated into behavior. There is one act par excellence which profanes money by going directly against the law of money, an act for which money is not made. This act is giving.[21]

This seems to be exactly what Jesus is saying. Giving money away shows that you are a slave to the God of grace, not to money. Jesus the fool creates a character who trusts in his master's goodness and helps others as he goes. Then he calls us to do the same.

Giving it to whom?

If giving money away is the very act for which it was *not* made, and if by doing so we remove its religious power over us, to whom exactly should we give it? Presumably, the poor. But who are the poor? This might seem like a ridiculous question, but it is more complex than one might think. In fact, an examination of poverty is essential for the proper de-sacralizing of money. If we profane money by giving it to those in need, then it is incumbent upon us to become familiar with the recipients of our giving. As Jacques Ellul says, "The power of money is not completely disgraced until we have seen what and who the poor are."[22]

Ashley Barker discusses this matter in *Make Poverty Personal*. He points out that the Greeks had only one word for the poor (*ptochoi*), which doesn't do justice to the varieties of poverty discussed in Scripture. However, the Hebrews had five different terms to describe the poor. A summary of these terms reveals the depth and breadth of poverty as understood in the Bible:

- *chacer*—those who lack something, as in those who are poor in wisdom, or poor in shelter or food.

- *ruwsh*—those who are dispossessed of land, possessions, or dignity.

- *dal*—those who are frail, weak, or helpless (the term most commonly translated as "the poor").

- *ebyown*—the needy, or those who depend on charity.

- *aniy*—those who are oppressed, exploited, or crushed by the powerful.

These terms appear throughout the Bible over 260 times. They show us the various facets of poverty in our world. Barker concludes,

> These words describe the marginalisation and oppression that the poor face, to the core of their very identity. The poor internalise their marginalisation and oppression. This affects their view of themselves and their place in the world. It makes them feel less than human.[23]

An acknowledgement of the presence of the poor is the first step in conquering the power of money. See them. Hear them. Listen to them. But a second step is required, and that involves seeing the poor as living representatives of Jesus himself. They are the permanent, constant reflection of Jesus the poor one. He told us that himself in a parable in Matthew 25 where he says that that which we do—or don't do—for the "least of these" (the hungry, the dispossessed, the naked, the imprisoned) we do—or don't do—for him. The poor then become God's question to us: will you feed, clothe, house, visit my Poor Son? This makes sense of Jesus' troubling words, "You will always have the poor with you, but you will not always have me" (Matthew 26:11). It is true that the Poor Son doesn't stay here on earth, but he leaves his representatives, his reflection.

At the risk of over-quoting Jacques Ellul, "The poor must be present among us to the end of the world in order to disturb our pride and our consciences by continually asking God's question of our lives."[24] It should follow then, that those of us who serve God as our true master, and not money, must become acquainted with the poor for it is among them that we will see Jesus.

St. Francis of Assisi was known for referring to the poor themselves as *sacramental*. A sacrament is a physical, tangible element through which the grace of Jesus can be experienced. The bread and wine in a communion feast is just ordinary bread and wine, but by faith we can experience a special unction or touch of God's grace when we eat and drink together in Jesus' name. Catholics during the time of St. Francis would have believed in seven sacraments—baptism, confession and penance, communion, confirmation, marriage, ordination, and the last rites. It was assumed that these external, visible ceremonies were the means by which certain graces are to be conferred on us. St. Francis went further. He suggested that since Jesus had declared himself in extreme solidarity with the "least of these" that the poor themselves were a means of experiencing God's presence. It's quite a radical idea today, as it was then. If we are looking for Jesus we can find him among the poor.

The practice of hospitality

But we need to be careful here that we don't just see this as a call to make donations to charity. Ash Barker rightly suggests, ". . . poverty can't be turned around simply by giving money, or even changing laws or political structures. It takes people full of hope and faith in Jesus to turn this despair around. . . ."[25] Jesus' foolish story of the cunning manager affirms two profound things—our salvation comes from God alone, and we are to relieve the suffering of others. One of the helpful ways to look at this is as a call to both accept and give *hospitality*. We are called to accept God's offer of hospitality and to show hospitality to others.

These days we seem to have boiled the powerful idea of hospitality down to the entertaining of friends in our home. While true hospitality might include dinner parties and overnight guests, it has a broader meaning. One writer alert to the biblical concept of hospitality was Henri Nouwen, who defined it as such: "Hospitality, therefore, means primarily the creation of a free space where the stranger can enter and become a friend instead of an enemy."[26] God creates such a space for us to become his friend. He also calls us to create such a space for others.

Nouwen believed that the defining spirit of our age is that of *hostility*. Our society, he said, is full of anxiety and fear, defensiveness and aggression, with each looking out for his own and increasingly suspicious of others. We are building walls around our property and viewing strangers as potential threats. During my first visit to New York City, I was informed by my hosts that when I rode the subway from their suburban home into Manhattan I must never make eye contact with any strangers. Shortly after, I saw a television program in which actors lay on busy sidewalks in major cities like New York, London, Paris, looking like they had passed out (or worse). A camera crew from across the street then filmed scores of people walking around the seemingly unconscious bodies, avoiding any contact with them. This is hostility at its worst. It took up to an hour in one city before any passer-by stopped to offer hospitality.

This, said Nouwen, is our task as Christians: to convert *hostis* into *hospis*, hostility into hospitality. In the ancient world hospitality was a firmly entrenched ethic. It was believed that God offered special protection to strangers and itinerants. Among both Jews and Gentiles it was believed that the failure to welcome strangers would incur divine wrath, while conversely, generous hospitality attracted blessings from above. This can be seen in Genesis 18 where Abraham welcomes a heavenly party, and in the following chapter where Sodom is punished for, among other things, their inhospitality. Even Jesus' words in Matthew 25 about "the least of these" refers to taking in the stranger, and in Acts 14, Paul and Barnabas find themselves the recipients of the excessive hospitality of the Lystrans who mistake the apostles for divine visitors.

During Jesus' time there had developed an underclass of needy people who would present themselves at the doors of the wealthy asking for a meal or a room for the night. These uninvited guests were taking advantage of the Mediterranean ethic for hospitality. Sometimes they were friends of an invited guest, or they would arrive at the same time as an invited guest, and so in the

Greco-Roman world they were called *umbrae*, or shadows. Over time this term was employed to refer to any uninvited guest: women, children, servants/slaves, outcasts like lepers, the poor, the disabled.

Earlier in this book, we saw how a woman presented herself uninvited to a meal Jesus was sharing at Simon the Pharisee's home. She was a classic umbrae, the invited guest shadowing Jesus. But Jesus himself acted as an umbrae when in Luke 19 he invited himself into the home of Zacchaeus the tax collector. In fact, as an itinerant, it is possible that Jesus was regularly in the position of an umbrae. If this is so, there could be no greater evidence for his status as a fool. We often picture Jesus, the one accused of being a drunkard and a glutton, as a legitimately invited guest of honor, but maybe it is closer to the truth that he was a lurker at kitchen doors, a shadow, reliant on the mercy of others.

If this is the case then it casts a completely different light on his teaching about hospitality. In Matthew 25, when Jesus talks about feeding the hungry, clothing the naked and accepting the stranger, he might well have been talking about himself in more than a spiritual or figurative way. It also makes sense of why the Pharisees were so offended by his eating habits and in particular his eating companions—other umbrae?

Poverty makes a good host

If, as Henri Nouwen suggests, hospitality involves the creation of a free and safe space for the fostering of friendship, then Jesus' words in Luke 16 about using money to make friends makes sense. But as long as we are suspicious of others or anxious about defending our own property or status, we can never truly be open to others. In this respect, Nouwen points out that we must become like the poor, like those with nothing to lose, to truly offer hospitality:

> Once we have become poor, we can be a good host. It is indeed a paradox of hospitality that poverty makes a good host.[27]

Notice how in Jesus' parable about the dishonest manager it is only when the manager is destitute that he finds the room to be interested in others. He is financially poor, but he is poor in spirit as well. All his defenses are gone and he finally has the capacity to offer hospitality to his clients *as equals.* We only look at strangers as enemies when we have something to defend. But it takes the poverty of Jesus to genuinely create a free and friendly space, a zone or a quality of relationship that allows the stranger, whether the poor in spirit or materially poor, to freely enter.

Jesus was poor. His is a refreshing poverty that allows him to accept others as one with nothing to lose. There are no defenses up with Jesus. Like a fool, too simple to know he shouldn't be so accepting, Jesus fashions free and friendly space around. This is a space that quickly fills up with "sinners"—women, children, lepers, tax collectors and others. It follows, then, that the church should essentially be a community of poor people. Paul says of the church in Corinth, "Not many of you were wise according to worldly standards, not many were powerful, not many were of noble birth" (1 Cor 1:26). It seems that he is presenting this statement to the Corinthians as an obvious fact and as a reference to the way things ought to be.

The church cannot be an assembly of the rich; it is made for poor outsiders. Jesus says so himself when he declares, "It is not the healthy who need a doctor, but the sick" (Mark 2:17). And he came to call the poor *outsiders.* In the parable of the feast, all these wretched ones were invited. The body of Christ, the body of the Poor One, can be composed only of the poor, not because they are superior, but simply because in their situation they are in accord with the person of Jesus Christ. This should be a constant sorrow to the members of our churches who are aware of it.

Jesus the fool would clearly object to targeted efforts to Christianize the powerful: millionaires, cabinet members, generals, company presidents. While it is perfectly possible for the powerful to experience God's grace in Christ, it is also true that they, like us all, must answer the question raised by the poor. Either they will stay powerful and the church will cease being a true church and their social influence will amount to nothing, or they will accept the strange and foolish call by Jesus to use their money to make friends.

So convinced of the need to embrace the poverty of Jesus was Henri Nouwen that he resigned his tenure as a professor at Yale University and moved into a group-home for intellectually disabled people as their caregiver. There he discovered that the intellectual "poverty" of his disabled clients made them superb hosts. In the last years of his life, Nouwen says he learned much about being a follower of Christ through his so-called clients. In fact, their hospitality renewed his faith.

If you've seen the harrowing 2004 film *Hotel Rwanda* you'll have seen the awesome power of hospitality in a world of depravity and evil. It tells the story of what happened in 1994 Rwanda when Hutus descended into a hell of bloodshed and racial violence against their Tutsi counterparts. Paul Rusesabagina, the temporary manager of the luxury hotel Mille Collines, sheltered over a thousand Tutsis from marauding death squads. Deserted by international peacekeepers, Rusesabagina, himself a Hutu, began cashing in every favor he had ever earned, bribing the Rwandan Hutu soldiers and keeping the bloodthirsty militia (mostly) outside the gates during the hundred days of slaughter during which nearly one million Rwandans were hacked to death by machetes. The international community turned their backs on Rwandan Tutsis, claiming they were powerless to help, but the story of Paul Rusesabagina suggests there was another possible path.

Rusesabagina used all his money to make friends. He was left a pauper by the end, but he provides us with a model for the very thing Jesus has been talking about. On April 15, 1994, a week after the genocide had began, Rusesabagina called for protection for those inside the Mille Collines in an interview with a Belgian newspaper. Likewise, an official of Sabena, the Belgian owners of the hotel, spoke on Belgian television on behalf of those sheltering in the Mille Collines. Rwandan authorities responded by posting some national police at the hotel.

Then on April 23 the Department of Military Intelligence arrived at the hotel and ordered Rusesabagina to turn out everyone who had sought shelter there. Rusesabagina and several of the occupants began telephoning influential persons abroad, appealing urgently for help. One of those who received a call was the Director General of the French Foreign Ministry. Before half an hour had elapsed, a colonel from the national police arrived to end the siege and to oblige the army to leave.

Then again on May 13 a captain came to the hotel to warn that there would be an attack on the hotel that afternoon. On that day, the French Foreign Ministry received a fax from the hotel saying that Rwandan government forces plan to massacre all the occupants of the hotel in the next few hours. It directed its representative at the UN to inform the secretariat of the threat and presumably also brought pressure to bear directly on authorities in Kigali, as others may have done also. The attack never took place.

In other words, the West had enough influence to save lives in Rwanda, but it used that influence only sparingly. Paul Rusesabagina provided one of the very few places of refuge, a haven of hospitality in a sea of depravity. None of the people who took shelter at the hotel was killed during the genocide. Rusesabagina's remarkable hospitality shames the ineffectual Western community who stood by while hundreds of thousands were killed. He fed and housed terrified Tutsis and against all odds saved every one of them. In recent years, leaders of national governments and international institutions have acknowledged their shortcomings in Rwanda. During a visit to Rwanda in 1998, President Clinton apologized for not acting. Kofi Annan, the UN Secretary General, said he personally could have done more to stop it.

But the genocide in Rwanda is not an isolated incident. After the Nazi Holocaust the international community pledged to never again allow genocide to take place. But it has happened—in places like Cambodia (under Pol Pot), the former Yugoslavia (under Milosovic), Rwanda, and most recently in Sudan's troubled Darfur region where more than 700,000 people have been killed or have died from hunger and disease. According to the UN another 1.5 million people have been displaced.

Was Christ the stranger or an angel hiding in the Mille Collines hotel in 1994? Is he slowly starving in the Darfur refugee camps? Who is showing hospitality? Who is opening their table to the hungry and the poor? As we've seen, hospitality is not just about a cup of tea and some sympathy. Hospitality is a powerful force that can stand against unspeakable evil. As followers of Jesus the fool, we should be at the forefront of offering hospitality to the hungry, to the refugee, to the dispossessed.

JESUS' OFFER TO THE FOOLHARDY

Student: Is it true, professor, you
believe that a paradox lies at the
very heart of the universe?
Professor: Well, yes and no.

arold Kushner is a rabbi who served the Temple Israel in Massachusetts. When asked by LIFE magazine what he thought was the meaning of life, he said he believed it is to be partners in creation with God. He illustrated this idea by telling the reporter that the Hebrews often ask why God didn't create trees that grow loaves of bread. Wouldn't that have made things much easier? But no, God created wheat so that humans may sow it, tend it, water it, harvest it, grind it, knead it, bake it and turn it into bread. In other words, God delights in people becoming his partners in creativity and production. I'll buy that.

My father often used to say that "God helps them that help themselves." In this approach to life, there is no room for God. There is nothing but human endeavor. God (if he exists in this perspective) looks on helplessly and hopelessly. But I meet a good many people who see every endeavor as a super-spiritual opportunity. Converse to my father's approach, they perceive life as being all God, with human beings looking on helplessly.

I knew a woman like this whose daughter attended our daughter's birthday party. When her child took a fall in our back yard and split her lip on the pathway, she scooped the screaming, bloodied girl into her arms and repeated over and over, "Praise the Lord! Praise the Lord! Praise the Lord!" Now I thought she was "praising the Lord" because no greater damage was done than a split lip, but some of our friends thought she was a nut case, thanking God for injuring her daughter. They thought she considered that every event was orchestrated by God and our only recourse was to thank him for keeping us safe when all was well or, when bad things happen, to thank him that they weren't worse.

Kushner's perspective that we are partners with God in creation, that we enter into a cooperative arrangement, allows for life to include both human and divine effort. Christians have often had the belief that God can get along very well without humans, thank you very much. In this way, Christians affirm their faith in an autonomous, independent God. But the fact of the matter is that, though God *can* get by without my help, that is not the way he prefers it. He would rather that he and I become partners in a productive, creative process called life. He didn't just create a loaf-of-bread-tree for me. He wants me to create bread out of the resources he has given me.

On the other hand, I could probably get by in life without God. Plenty of other people manage it. They go through life without any reference to God whatsoever. I suppose I could. Technically. But this is not the way I prefer it. I would rather walk shoulder-to-shoulder with God, knowing that life is far more satisfying, productive, and therapeutic with him than without him.

So what does this satisfying, creative, healthy lifestyle look like when it is actually lived out? Is there a model for living like God's partner against which I can measure my progress (or at times, my lack of progress)? Well, there is. But a lot of people get alarmed by someone who imagines they are on a mission from God. Those who think they are God's special agents invariably get crushed in this world and probably for good reason: most of them are insane. So who would risk being fool enough to think they are partners with God? Only the truly foolish ones.

American Christian essayist Phyllis Theroux once wrote:

> Many years ago I took a Civil Service entrance exam that contained certain questions designed to sort out the people who had "Messiah complexes" or thought that J. Edgar Hoover was giving them varicose veins. Those questions were easy to spot, although the only one that still sticks in my mind is "Do you think you are a special agent of God?" I paused, thought about all the government benefits which hung upon the answer, and wrote, "No." I would like to think that, under the same circumstances, Mr. Hoover might have lied, too.[28]

We might think it a little presumptuous to consider ourselves in league with the Creator of heaven and earth, but deep down we know that only as God's partners can we live with a sense of destiny and significance. Jesus was fool enough to believe that he was on such a mission from God. As I said, you have to be a fool to dare to believe it of yourself. But Jesus demonstrated time and again that he was the most exquisite example of human and divine in partnership. Look at him. Rediscover the biblical picture of Jesus and see what a foolish lifestyle looks like. In our short survey of his clever reframing style, we have learned something about this strange and wonderful man. I hope you can agree with me when I say that the world could do with more fools like Jesus. In order to systematize our thinking, consider the following points about the foolishness of Christ.

Jesus realistically describes our limitations

M. Scott Peck uses very creatively the illustration of one of the most common myths throughout history to describe human nature. The myth he draws upon is that of the dragon. Stories about dragons have been told by Christians, Jews, Muslims, Buddhists, and Hindus in every one of the major epochs of history. So what is it about dragons that seems to gel with the common experience of men and women no matter what their religious perspective or their place in history?

Peck suggest that dragon imagery has been so popular because dragons are potent symbols of what human nature is like. A dragon is nothing more than a snake with wings. And as a snake with wings, it illustrates what we humans are really like. We are like serpents inasmuch as we are capable of the most low and depraved acts ever encountered in the animal kingdom. Humans are able to demonstrate remarkably base, primal behavior that suggests we are the most savage of all creatures. And yet, like a dragon, we have the wings to fly above our limitations, to soar over our coarse urges and be capable of the most noble acts of sacrifice, love, grace, and mercy.

This is the ultimate paradox of being human; we bear the potential for graphic acts of evil and yet we are made in the image of God and bear the potential to ignite the spark of divinity within us. We are snakes with wings.

It is this very reality that Jesus the fool highlights for us. Many religions belabor the wretchedness of humankind. Others bear heavily on human godliness. Jesus is foolish enough to recommend the paradox. He can understand that we are made by God in his image and are potentially capable of being the human temple of God's Spirit. But he can also be very decisive about human sin.

Remember Jesus' clever use of the story about the Good Samaritan? It reminds us that even though we are capable of acts of mercy, it is simply beyond us to love perfectly. The inability to love enough (no matter how well we may love) is the basis of sin. Sin, if you remember, is the falling short of a standard of perfection. It is not about a perfect God creating an imperfect humankind and then setting a perfect standard that he knew we could not reach, like some cosmic joke on people. Instead, it is about creatures who have the potential for evil and the potential for purity, but who are always predisposed to choose evil. Do I have to create a great catalogue of the despicable acts of indecency that humans have inflicted upon themselves? Surely not. Read tonight's newspaper. Visit any one of the memorials around the globe that reside as testimonies to human inhumanity.

I have a friend who recently visited the memorial to the excesses of Nazism at Auschwitz. He said you cannot walk through that God-forsaken place without feeling putrid to your very bones. Among his tour party was a young German girl who, upon seeing the hundreds of kilograms of human hair collected from the gassed corpses, ran from the building sobbing.

The serial killings of Jeffrey Dahmer in Milwaukee reminded us that human evil is not necessarily confined to the great organized genocide conducted by the Nazis. Dahmer appeared to be capable of the most horrific and unthinkable acts of indecency ever perpetrated by an individual. I can remember seeing excerpts of his trial in which the prosecuting lawyer raised the interesting discovery that Dahmer had not committed any acts of atrocity, nor had he even committed a misdemeanor against any local ordinances, during a two-year period from 1982 to 1984. The prosecutor wanted to know why that was the case. Dahmer responded from the witness box that during that period he was living with his grandmother and going to church every week. He was also reading his Bible regularly.

But the prosecutor pressed him. He wanted to know what happened in 1984 to trigger the worst phase of his behavior. And Dahmer's response was chilling. He simply said, "In 1984, my compass broke." Initially, I wasn't sure what he was talking about. Was he so insane that when his old Boy Scout compass packed it in he went on a killing spree? The prosecutor inquired further. What Dahmer meant was that his conscience suddenly ceased to function. He no longer knew the difference between right and wrong. What causes such dysfunction I can't begin to imagine. My point, however, is that Jeffrey Dahmer is right. We all have a built-in compass that keeps us aware of the difference between right and wrong. When it breaks, we become capable of inordinate evil.

Jesus reframes a view of sin that imagines it is simply the con-travening of a particular moral code. Sin is endemic to the human condition. When we compromise our commitment to the truth our response is usually, "I told a lie." But Jesus reframes it as "I am a liar." It says something about our very nature as humans rather than about our ability to keep certain rules or regulations. We are snakes. As noble and as merciful as we might imagine ourselves to be, the Good Samaritan points out just how costly and difficult it is to fulfill a regulation like "Love your neighbor as yourself."

There were times when Jesus was prepared to be quite blunt in his approach to sin. In Matthew 5:21–22 he is reported to have made it quite clear that there is more to the human condition than following or breaking rules and laws. He said: "You have heard it said to people long ago, 'Do not murder, anyone who murders will be subject to judgment.' But I tell you that anyone who is angry with his brother will be subject to judgment." In other words, it's possible to go through life and never actually murder anyone. But don't think that makes you perfect. If you've ever wished evil, pain, suffering, or death on anyone, you stand condemned.

In the same vein he goes on in verses 27 and 28: "You have heard it was said, 'Do not commit adultery.' But I tell you that any-one who looks at a woman lustfully has already committed adul-tery with her in his heart." Again, its is possible to go through life and remain physically faithful to your spouse. But Jesus turns the cold light of day on a person's inner thoughts. Ever looked upon someone else as a physical object whose purpose is purely to gratify your appetites? Such arrogance is as sinful as if you had slept with someone other than your spouse, says Jesus.

Even more fantastically he suggests in verses 43 and 44: "You have heard it said, 'Love your neighbor an hate your enemy.' But I tell you: 'Love your enemies and pray for those who persecute you.'" Jesus reframes our perception of sin. If being sinless was just the keeping of a particular regimen there is the chance some of us could manage it and some could not, depending on our personal degree of discipline. Why, Paul was able to say, ". . . as for legalistic righteousness [I was] faultless" (Philippians 3:6). He was able to boast that when it came to following rules, he was perfect. But he knew that that didn't necessarily make him perfect. It may have made him disciplined. But not perfect.

Jesus dramatically said that a truly faultless life involves never thinking ill of your brother. It involves never looking at a person with lust in your eyes. It involves loving your enemies and praying for them. What do I hear you say? That's impossible? Exactly. When Jesus pronounced those sayings I've recounted above, he didn't do so in order to suggest that you can't come to him unless you never think another evil thought. Far from it. He said them to remind people that on the outside we can put on a good show. But it was imperative to Jesus that we be under no illusions as to what we are really like. Deep down we know we are not right. Our compasses keep prompting us with that fact if we are normal, healthy human beings.

If we are to develop new pictures of Jesus, we had better take into account that we need a very realistic view of what we are like. The Fool was pretty canny. There is no fooling the Fool when it comes to human inadequacy.

I've heard someone relate Malcolm Muggeridge's sordid story of how, when he was a journalist in India, he had grown weary of his wife and determined to take a lover. He concocted various scenarios about how such a sexual conquest might be consummated. One day, he was swimming in a river when he spied a woman across the waters on the opposite bank. She was alone and naked and appeared attractive and inviting from his vantage point. He resolved that this was it. There was no one within sight. He decided to take her as his lover.

Swimming across the river, he casually drew nearer and nearer the object of his unbridled lust. Within feet of her, he bobbed under the water and glided towards the bank. When he broke forth from beneath the surface, he found himself barely inches from her. Their eyes met and each of them gasped in horror. She was a leper. It had shocked her that a white man—or any man—had come so close. But for Muggeridge it was a gruesome and tragic reminder of his own depravity. He had tried to convince himself all the way across the river that it was her lecherous body that was propelling him towards her. But upon seeing her so closely, he realized it was his own lecherous heart that was driving him. He had been victim to his own sin.

Likewise, the same Paul who could claim that he was faultless according to the laws of Judaism, also called himself in 1 Timothy 1:15 the "chief of sinners." This is the first step in becoming a partner with God: being prepared to be more realistic about your own inadequacy. It took Jesus the fool to really make it clear to me.

Jesus shows us how to rise above our limitations

Remember the mythical symbol of the dragon? It reminds us that we are snakes. But dragons are snakes that can fly. And within human beings is the irresistible urge to soar above the limitations of our "snake-ness" (if there is such a word!) and to take to the wing. In other words, we need to know that our sin can be canceled.

I remember seeing an episode of "A Current Affair" that concerned a young man who was driving home one afternoon having drunk too much and who lost control of his vehicle and killed a little girl. He was charged with manslaughter and found guilty and, after the judge took into account his previously unblemished record, was put on a good behavior bond for a few years. Well, the parents of the dead girl were outraged. How could the life of their daughter be worth so little? Believing that justice had not been done, they decided to pursue the matter through the courts. Now he had already been found guilty and so could not be charged and retried for the same crime. So the parents decided to sue him for damages incurred by the loss of their child. The case went back to court and a judge had to fix a sum to be paid by the youth to the parents of the girl.

The judge's decision was so quirky that it made all the network news programs take notice. The young man was to pay the plaintiffs one dollar a week for some considerable number of years. I don't remember what the final sum would have worked out to be, but it was the method of payment that I will never forget. He had to write a check for one dollar, made out in the name of the deceased child, and pay it on the day of the week that he had killed her (I think it was on a Friday he made his dreadful mistake). So can you imagine every Friday writing a check for a dollar in the name of the child whose life you had ended? You as the listener sense the parent's grief at their loss. You almost taste their frustration at the boy's light sentence. You engage in their anger as they pursue him through the legal system. When the horrific judgment regarding compensation is announced, there is almost relief that this morbid business is finished.

Then the unthinkable happened. After a few months, the boy stopped making the payments. "A Current Affair" is pretty good at manipulating the emotions and the viewer's first response is one of outrage. Why couldn't this man even manage one dollar a week? Then the reporter went to the youth to get his side of the story. We only met him in the final stages of the report. As he faced the camera, he sobbed with an uncontrollable remorse and through his tears he wailed: "It's not having to pay a dollar that I object to. In fact, I'll pay anything. I'll spend the rest of my life in prison. I'd sacrifice anything rather than write those checks." His eloquence was shattering as he explained that those checks were a constant reminder to him that he wasn't yet, and never would be, forgiven of his mistake. "I just want to know that they forgive me!" he wept. "I would do anything for that." And yet when the reporter returned to the parents, it was clear they had no intention of doing any such thing. At the end of the TV segment, they were taking him back to court!

I tell that story because it graphically illustrates how paralyzing it is to know that you are condemned to be a snake forever. We have an inbuilt need to be able to fly above the horrible truths of human frailty. The foolishness of Jesus' understanding is that however unlikely it might seem, there is forgiveness in and through him. The parable of the two debtors that he told to Simon the Pharisee is an encapsulation of his thinking on this point. No matter who we are, whether we have committed the most heinous crimes or whether we are decent law-abiding citizens, we all have a need to know that our mistakes, our inadequacy, our frailties can be forgiven. Only forgiveness sets us free to fly.

I've heard Ravi Zacharias, the Indian-born evangelist, tell of an experience he had in Calcutta where a good many people worship Kali, the goddess of protection. Walking through the crowded back streets, he encountered a priest dressed all in white about to perform a sacrifice. As he watched, Zacharias observed a man come forward carrying a goat. The priest placed the goat's neck in a crude device and with a swift blow severed its head from its convulsing body. The dusty street was splattered with the ribbon of blood that spewed forth. Then the man who was making absolution, the one who presented the goat in the first place, placed his own head in the sacrificial device for a few seconds. He then smeared himself all over with the goat's blood and left quickly. Zacharias tried to find out from the priest what was going on but was told to mind his own business.

I see this story as an acting out of the universal longing for absolution, for forgiveness. Jesus the fool recognized this longing and offered the prescription for our malady. The only way to satisfy that craving is by the cross. God forgives a forgiveness-hungry people through the remarkable mystery of Jesus' sacrifice on the cross. The story of Ahmed Shah's dilemma between love and justice very clearly illustrates our way of absolution. We deserve to be cast from God's sight because of our sin, but based on his unquenchable love for us he creatively found another way. If you want to become one of God's partners, the only way is to recognize his grace in allowing Jesus to die in order to set you free from the penalty normally imposed on a sinful humankind.

Bono from U2 describes the scandal of grace this way:

> . . . at the center of all religions is the idea of karma. You know, what you put out comes back to you: an eye for an eye, a tooth for a tooth, or in physics, every action is met by an equal or an opposite one. It's clear to me that karma is at the very heart of the universe. I'm absolutely sure of it. And yet, along comes this idea of grace to upend all that "as you reap, so you will sow" stuff. Grace defies reason and logic. Love interrupts, if you like, the consequences of your actions, which in my case is very good news indeed, because I've done a lot of stupid stuff.[29]

And yet the cross seems such an awkward way forward. Paul was so keenly aware of the offense that that device of torture could cause to thinking adults. How can the cross, of all things, be the way of absolution? This is the most supremely foolish aspect of Jesus' life and work. The atonement in the cross is a mysterious concept to fathom. C. S. Lewis just couldn't understand how there was atonement in so primitive a symbol as the cross of Calvary. What has the crucifixion of a man named Jesus two thousand years ago got to do with the forgiveness of our sins? Lewis tried every way to understand it as a theological/philosophical concept.

Finally, he recognized his need simply to risk living as though it was so and noticed the dramatic impact it had on his life. This is how he described his decision to adopt faith in the cross for absolution:

> The choice appeared to be momentous, but it was also strangely unemotional. I was moved by no desires or fears. In a sense, I was not moved by anything. I chose to open, to unbuckle, to loosen the rein. I say "I chose," yet it did not really seem possible to do the opposite. On the other hand, I was aware of no motives. You can argue that I was not a free agent, but I am inclined to think that this came nearer to being a perfectly free act than most I have ever done.[30]

Jesus, like the sacrificial goat in Calcutta, is the payment for our sins. The theological term is "propitiation." But don't let that word put you off. Propitiation is the process of making an offering to appease a disgruntled god. And in a sense the God of the Christians is a disgruntled god. He is disgruntled with our sin. The offering of a sacrifice puts things right. Now God chooses to put things right with the ultimate sacrifice: he allows himself, in the form of a man, to be destroyed for the sin of the world. Understand? I don't blame you if you don't. How can an eternal God be destroyed? That's why I find C. S. Lewis' testimony of how he "unbuckled" or "loosened the rein" so helpful. When his powers of understanding could no longer cope with such a mind-boggling concept, he simply had to let go and risk living as though it was all true.

I meet many people who want to have faith but who cannot seem to muster it from within. One man I met wanted to know if there was a potion you could take to bring on an attack of faith. Although he was joking, there was a great deal of truth to his yearning. But ultimately there will always remain an element of mystery surrounding matters of spirituality. I've never been to the South Pole, but I still believe it's there. It doesn't take much faith to believe it. But faith in God's grace as revealed by Jesus takes some doing. It's not meant to be easy or it wouldn't be faith. There has to be some sacrifice on our part.

The cross causes some intellectual problems to those struggling to find faith; it also seems to arouse the resistance of even the most faithful. I think it has something to do with our refusal to accept forgiveness at so great a cost. If I know I am forgiven and all that it cost me was the life of a single goat, I can't see any reason to resist. But when the price of forgiveness is the life of the most wonderful and whimsical human being ever to walk the earth, it is harder to take.

In Matthew's Gospel there are a couple of episodes that illustrate what I mean. As Jesus was about to come to the cross, he asked his disciples who they thought he was. There were several well-meaning answers given until Peter said, "You are the messiah, the Son of the living God."[31] Jesus applauded Peter's perception by telling him that he couldn't have worked out so great a mystery all by himself. It could only be understood as revealed by God's Spirit. So, well done, Peter, for being open to what God wanted to reveal to you! Then, believing his disciples (and probably especially Peter) to be ready for an even greater truth, he told them that when he got to Jerusalem he would be tortured and crucified for the sins of humanity. At this point, Peter said, "No way, lord! This will never happen to you."[32] Can you imagine Jesus throwing his arms up in frustration? Peter, at one moment, had discovered half the secret of this man named Jesus: that he was the Messiah. But in the next moment, he had refused to believe the other half of the secret: that the Messiah must suffer and die for the forgiveness of sins.

Such is our resistance to the cross. We can enjoy the foolishness of Jesus through his delightful stories and his whimsical manner. But when it comes to torture and death, we pull up short. Surely not. Surely Jesus didn't die for us. It's easier to believe he was destroyed by the cynical, self-righteous arrogance of the rulers of this world than it is to see him as the sacrificial animal on the altar.

But paradoxically, we seem to need to feel forgiven at almost any cost. I've heard about a television program in which a man dies and finds himself in the waiting room with two large doors marked "heaven" and "hell." There is a disinterested usher sitting between them reading the paper. He looks up and says, "Oh listen, we're pretty busy today. Why don't you just choose a door and go on through?"

The man who has just died is aghast. "You mean, just go on through?" he says. "What about judgment and stuff like that?"

"Oh, no need to bother with that," replies the usher. "Just choose a door."

"But you mean there's no reckoning, no accounting for my life? What about a judgment?"

"Look," says the usher, annoyed, "there are people dying and lining up behind you. Just choose a door!"

And so at the end of the story, the newly-deceased man chooses the door to hell. The point of the story is that we all *want* to give an account. We *want* a day of reckoning. Of course, there's an element of excitement in getting away with something, but even deeper down we desire to be judged for our choices, whether good or poor. The Fool suggests that we can have our day of reckoning and still encounter freedom through forgiveness. But it takes faith. How much, you ask? A little more than none at all.

Snakes that can fly

If you truly desire to be a partner with God, you are called to believe two apparently contradictory ideas. First, you are a snake, a sinner, incapable of finding God's favor. Second, you can fly, knowing the extraordinary worth with which God sees you and on the basis of which he forgives you. In other words, you are a dragon.

These two opposing concepts, held in tension, make up the core of the Christian faith. There will be times in our lives when we appear to be more keenly aware of one concept than the other. I meet people who seem to be profoundly aware of their sin. They think they are putrid and rotten to the core. And they are right. But they are not yet fit to be partners with God. I also meet lots of people (mainly from churches) who can tell you in detail about their forgiveness and their new life. They are keenly aware that they are free to fly above their limitations. And they are right. But they are not yet fit to be partners with God.

The rock singer Sting once said:

> I think we're all capable of becoming the worst—the child molester, the thief. Not to admit it is to go mad. We must steer a middle course and say, "Yes, I have this potential. But I also have the opposite po-

tential, to be St. Francis of Assisi." We have Genghis Khan on one side and St. Francis on the other and to steer a course between the two is sanity.[33]

Becoming one of God's true agents involves being keenly aware of *both* these understandings at the same time. When we can learn the balance of holding both truths in tension, then we are one of God's useful partners. I realize that there are periods of our lives when we are far more aware of our snake-ness than we are of our ability to fly. And there are times in our journeys when we are soaring way above our sin on wings of forgiveness. But our goal in the Christian walk is to develop balance. It's like a pendulum swinging between awareness of forgiveness on one side and awareness of sinfulness on the other. At certain points in our lives it will swing violently in one direction or the other. But Christian maturity means minimizing the swing and learning to hold both types of awareness in tension. And that struggle may take a lifetime. In fact, I'm yet to meet someone who has mastered it. Nevertheless, it remains a tremendous ideal after which to strive.

Jesus is invariably critical of religious people who have no balance between the concept of their sinfulness and that of their forgiveness. Simon the Pharisee was one example. Another is found in the story Jesus told about a Pharisee and a tax collector in Luke 18:9–14. In fact, Luke explains that Jesus was telling it to a group of people who "were confident of their own righteousness." In other words, they had no balance!

Jesus' story involves a Pharisee and a tax collector going to the Temple to pray. Remember that the Pharisees were the upholders of the traditions of Israel, and tax collectors were traitors who had sold out their commitment to those traditions, who had gone into league with the conquering Roman pagans to extract taxes from their Jewish brethren to fill the coffers in Rome. So these two represented, on the one hand, the most holy section of the community and, on the other, the most wretched. The squeaky clean and the thoroughly filthy!

The Pharisee stood up to pray, as was the custom. In the Temple, while the sacrifice was being carried out by the priests, it was not uncommon for those gathered to all pray out loud at the same time. There would have been a cacophony of prayers filling the Temple. The Pharisee prayed, "Thank you, God, that I am not like other men—robbers, evildoers, adulterers—or even like this tax collector! I fast twice a week and give a tenth of all I get." As you can clearly see, there is no balance in this man.

On the other hand, the tax collector could not bear to lift his head. He beat his chest (the chest, being the center of the body, was considered to be the seat of all emotion) and wailed, "God, have mercy on me, a sinner." In the one breath, he has acknowledged his inadequacy and appropriated God's forgiveness. Jesus ended his parable with the radical reframe "I tell you that this tax collector, rather than the Pharisee, went home justified before God."

The statement is a reframe, because Jesus' listeners would never have imagined a social outcast like a tax collector to be favored more highly by God than a holy man like the Pharisee. The difference between the two men in the story, however, is that one had no balance and the other had found a balance between the apparently conflicting ideas of sin and redemption. The tax collector is truly a dragon—a snake that can fly.

The foolish wisdom of Jesus

The struggle to find and maintain that balance is a monumental task, adopted by only the most foolhardy. Only the foolhardy know the greater joy that comes as you embrace the tension. As a matter of fact, the closer you come to these understandings, the more the foolishness of the cross inspires your soul. So Jesus first reframes our perception of sin and forgiveness. He reframes for us a perspective in which sin is not the doing of wrong things; it is the very nature of humanity. Sin is a condition that limits and retards our growth towards maturity, towards perfection. We saw him do this chiefly through the telling of the story of the Good Samaritan.

Second, he reframes our perception of forgiveness. It is not the earned right of a faithful follower of some religious system. It is God's offer of grace and love, a free gift in the form of a cross. The parable of the two debtors, whose debts were canceled, illustrates this reframe.

The next step we took was to recognize that there needs to be a level of balance in the tension between these two reframes. I believe that as we discover this balance we are inspired to live new lives as God's partners and produce something creative and worthwhile in our lives and the lives of those around us.

Remember the prostitute who decided to anoint Jesus' feet in the home of one of the holiest men in Israel? What a remarkably in-spired decision she made to express her newly-found dignity in that way! I have met many people, like her, who were trapped in situations that bound them and retarded their growth as individuals, but who upon encountering the Fool were inspired to better things, to shake off shackles that should never have limited them in the first place.

In the two other parables that we looked at we noticed a couple of the aspects of what this new, creative, and inspired life resembles. This balanced life sets us free from the superstition and greed that results from thinking that we can buy God's favor. As his servants, we live in the security of his eternal patronage (the parable of the obedient servant). Furthermore, we are freed from the insecurity of having to compete continually with our brothers and sisters for our place in the sun. The rewards of discovering this balance are greater acceptance and intimacy in human relationships (the parable of the rich fool). Security rests in knowing one's worth, in trusting the ac-ceptance of others and, ultimately, in trusting the love of God who knows us completely.

I hope you can see how the world really could do with more fools like Jesus! He has reframed so many of our preconceptions that the truth is liberating. It has often been mentioned that only a remarkable person like Jesus could have taught that mismatched group of disciples to love each other. In that community of twelve one of them was a zealot, a fanatical nationalist committed to the overthrow of the Roman oppressors (Simon), and another of them was a tax collector (Matthew). I've already mentioned the way tax collectors were viewed. They were the traitors who had sold out to the Romans. Only an extraordinary new dynamic could have brought these two together as brothers!

Zealots were noted for concealing daggers in the folds of their robes. With stealth they would sidle up to Roman soldiers or tax collectors or Roman officials in crowds and stab them silently. It was not unusual for a crowd to disperse and for a corpse to be left lying in the dust. For this reason, Roman collaborators rarely gathered in large crowds. In fact, there is a story in Luke's Gospel about a tax collector named Zacchaeus who, being somewhat short, shimmies up a tree to see Jesus through a crowd. But I wonder whether his lack of stature was the only reason for him being up that tree!

By discovering the balance that Jesus brings, Simon the Zealot and Matthew the tax collector learned to be brothers. And so did a rag-tag bunch of fishermen, farmers, whores, doctors, religious leaders, Greeks, Jews, Romans, Samaritans, blacks, whites, northerners, southerners, the educated, the illiterate, the sophisticated and the gullible.

When we learn to work on mastering the balance between our sinfulness and our self-worth, we find new reserves for living differently. Learning to embrace the foolishness of Jesus is worth the effort.

JESUS, THE FOOL WHO WON'T GIVE UP

I lose my head
From time to time
I make a fool of myself
In matters of the heart.
—Tracy Chapman

We have noted two distinct aspects to the foolishness of Jesus. First, we looked at his whimsical, uncomplicated approach to life and relationships. Second, we saw him reframe the conventional wisdom of his (and our) world by exploring his understandings of sin, forgiveness, and newness in relationships between us and God and amongst ourselves.

Loyalty as foolishness

Alastair Campbell called these two aspects "folly as simplicity" and "folly as prophecy." There is one further way of observing Jesus' foolishness. Campbell's name for it: "folly as loyalty." It takes a fool to live out that dogged, unrelenting loyalty even to those who continually reject them. I have encountered several parents who have had to remain committed to their teenage offspring even though their children have all but spat in their face. Invariably, they say to me something like: "I feel like a fool. I know my child is just treating me like a doormat, walking all over me, taking advantage of me. But I have such love that I can't give up."

This isn't to suggest that the time never comes when parents have to communicate to their adult sons or daughters that they are not prepared to be put through such abuse any longer and to draw some distinct boundaries. That is altogether healthy in the process of allowing them to grow up as responsible men or women. But the love that demands our steadfast loyalty to our children often has us feeling foolish when they chose to reject that love.

It is the same in any significant relationship. To remain loyal to the ones we love and to allow them the freedom to reject that love allows the potential to be made a fool of. Tracy Chapman, a profoundly affecting folk-poet, expresses this in a song called "Matters of the Heart."[34] The song is an eloquent expression of how stupid you feel when you have given love and kept giving love even when it has been rejected. This is the kind of foolishness we often see in the man called Jesus. He is so loyal, so devoted, so unshakable that it is embarrassing. He just won't give up.

In this regard, I find him very masculine. I know that God is neither male nor female and it's only our male-orientedness that prescribes that we call God "him." In fact, there are very many qualities about God that usually considered feminine in our culture. Jesus as God is nurturing, visceral, accepting, and intuitive. But in this area, he is particularly masculine. Like a lover who won't be spurned, he keeps coming back. He will pursue us until we are his. He, like God, really is the Hound of Heaven. This is the way the poet Francis Thompson imagined God: as a relentless seeker of those he loves. And Thompson had good reason to see God this way. He had run from God for most of his life until the dogged loyalty of the Hound finally caught him.

Born in England in 1859, Thompson was educated for the Catholic priesthood, but found reason to run and refused to pursue ordination. Rather, he took up medicine at Owens College, Manchester. But again he ran, dropping out of studies and ending up an opium addict in London. He became a vagrant, existing in the underworld society of Charing Cross. Still the Hound pursued him. Desperately drug-afflicted, he wrote a stirring poem about the Madonna and sent it to an editor called Wilfred Meynell who published a leading Catholic magazine. Meynell could not but recognize the sincerity of its author and published it. He then set about on a quest to find the poet who had sent the grubby, scribbled note to him.

Discovering the derelict Francis Thompson in Charing Cross, Meynell and his wife spent the rest of Thompson's life caring for him and acting as patrons to his talent. As much as he may have run, through the selfless love of the Meynells, God had finally tracked him down. He is now almost solely remembered for the poem, published in 1893, that he called "The Hound of Heaven." It has the hectic intensity of the pursued fugitive that you often find in the work of other opium-afflicted poets:

I fled Him, down the nights and down the days;
I fled Him, down the arches of the years;
I fled Him, down the labyrinthine ways
Of my own mind; and in the mist of tears
I hid from Him, and under running laughter.
Up vistaed hopes I sped;
And shot, precipitated,
Adown Titanic glooms of chasmed fears,
From those strong Feet that followed, followed after.
But with unhurrying chase,
And unperturbed pace,
Deliberate speed, majestic instancy,
They beat—and a Voice beat
More instant than the Feet—
"All things betray thee, who betrayest Me"

I can almost hear the pounding of the Hound's feet as he chases his quarry down. But it is his tender voice that reminds me that I can never be truly me, that I will always betray myself, until

I yield to him. The poem concludes in resigned acceptance of the pursuing God:

Ah, fondest, blindest, weakest,
I am he whom thou seekest!
Thou dravest love from thee, who dravest me.[35]

Interestingly, it has been my experience that those who seem to run from God the fastest are often the ones who feel the most pursued. I was once outside a hall where an evangelist was speaking and a young man was hanging around near the door. I suggested that he go in and hear what the preacher had to say.

"No thanks," came the reply. "I know if I go in I'll yield to God and I'm just not ready for it yet!" He knew that the message of God's love was irresistible to him and the only way not to respond was not to listen. I don't have trouble believing that the Hound of Heaven didn't have to pursue him much longer.

Jesus is like the hound before which Francis Thompson fell. His relentless, dogged unquenchable love for us is so loyal that invariably he will track us down. By this I don't mean that we have no choice, that faith in Jesus is a foregone conclusion. His love is so devoted that he allows us the choice to reject it. And this is what makes Jesus a fool. When everyone else has deserted us, the Fool remains unshakable.

Alastair Campbell illustrates this point with a reference to Shakespeare's *King Lear*. When Lear refused the genuine loyalty of Cordelia and Kent in preference to the treachery of Goneril, Regan, and Edmund, he began his descent into madness. (Note that a reframe regarding the motives of these latter three characters would have saved the situation from tragedy!) Cast out into the storm, the near-lunatic king found that his only companion was the fool. Why did the fool remain when everyone else had betrayed him? He did so to finally prove his worth. In contrast to the greed and treachery that have destroyed Lear, the fool presents the model of persistent, honest loyalty. Says Campbell:

*This enigma—the strange willingness to disregard self out of a higher loy-
alty—can be found at the center of Jesus' life and death.*[36]

Nowhere is this loyalty more poignantly presented than in Jesus'
anguish in the Garden of Gethsemane. After his last meal with his
closest compatriots, Jesus, perhaps anxious and fidgety, couldn't sit
still. He knew his final hours were approaching. So he took the
night air with his disciples down through the Kidron valley to a
garden containing olive trees east of where the current Jericho road-
bridge lies. It was a favorite retreat of Jesus and his disciples. There
in the solitude of the quiet evening, Jesus emotionally fell apart. He
disappeared to a darkened corner of the garden with his closest
friends—James, his brother John, and Peter—and there he broke
down and cried, inviting the prayers of his companions. But it was
late and they clearly didn't share their master's sense of apprehension.
The fell asleep on him during his darkest moment.

Alone and frightened, lying face down on the ground, Jesus
sobbed, "I'm so overwhelmed with sorrow that I could die." Clearly
this was a man beside himself with anguish. And here lies the key
to understanding the loyalty of the fool called Jesus. It seems to me
that it was here in this pretty garden that Jesus' faith was most sorely
tested. And he almost cracked! He was filled with fear and uncertainty and for this one moment his resolve was almost shattered.[37]

You might find it distressing to imagine Jesus falling apart at
the seams, but for me this is inspirational. If we imagine Jesus to be
always perfectly in control, to know all, to see all, to be steely in his
resolve and unflinching in his mission, we can never believe that
such things as fear or uncertainty were part of his experience. But
Gethsemane reminds us that they were. And the fact that they were
fills me with courage.

If Jesus was always completely certain of the outcome of his
life—if he knew everything that was to happen before it happened
and if he had no doubt about his final vindication—then where is
there room for faith? How can we talk about the faith of Jesus if

he was always aware of the events of every next moment? If he was completely and thoroughly sure, without the shadow of any doubt, that after his trial, humiliation, torture, and death, he would be resurrected to the right hand of God and all power both in heaven and on earth was to be given to him, there would be no need for him to exercise faith. And Gethsemane would not make sense. The events in that garden can only be sensible if there was an element of risk involved. Faith is risk. And at Gethsemane, Jesus showed he was faced with a terrible risk—the offering of his own life.

The fact that he was prepared to, in spite of his fears, go through with his commitment to be sacrificed for our inadequacy makes the cross the supreme symbol of faith. Not only do we place our faith in it, but we celebrate Jesus' faith that drove him to it. Gethsemane is proof that Jesus was undoubtedly foolish. Here he was, an innocent man, prepared to stick to his decision to go to the cross out of loyalty to his God and to this world. His dogged, relentless loyalty was shaken in that small garden, but it didn't fall. Like the Hound of Heaven who has chased his quarry up hill and down dale, Jesus paused at the very end of his quest and took stock. Nearly out of strength and afraid beyond belief, he nevertheless continued the hunt right to the bitter end. There's no one as loyal as the Fool.

This reminds me of a story seen recently on television during the telecast of the British sheepdog trials. Have you ever watched sheepdog trials? Contrary to what you might expect, they make fascinating television. A shepherd has to instruct his dog to complete a series of maneuvers with a group of three or four sheep. The dog has to round them into a pen or move them across to the other side of a paddock. Each of the dogs is timed and judged on efficiency and speed.

During one championship, the winning dog and his shepherd/ master appeared on camera to accept the trophy, and the television reporter stuck his microphone in the owner's mouth and asked him about how he felt at this his greatest moment. The characteristically taciturn Yorkshireman responded self-effacingly with nods and grunts. Then the interviewer pointed out that there was a tragic story behind this dog that had just won the British championship and asked the man to tell us about it. The craggy-faced old shepherd broke down as he told the tale.

It turned out that the old man had nursed this dog on his kitchen table for weeks and weeks after it had broken both its legs and had a hip replacement. So you can see how winning the British championship in sheepdog trialing was quite a monumental effort. But the interviewer pressed him further. What had happened to the dog?

And so the dog's owner repeated the story of how he had ordered his dog to sit by the shed until he returned from mending a fence on top of a nearby hill. His dog was so obedient that, once told to stay, he would never budge from that spot. As the shepherd worked on the fence, he heard the dog down by the shed begin to whine and squeal. He wondered what the problem was but went on with his work. Soon, he noticed the dog glancing anxiously behind the shed at something out of the shepherd's sight. The dog was looking longingly at his master, so the old man decided to wander down and see what was happening behind the shed. On his way down, he realized too late that one of his farm hands was driving a tractor out from behind the shed and heading slowly for the dog. Unable to see the animal and unable to hear the shepherd's screams, the farm worker drove right over the dog, crushing his hind legs and hips.

Tears were streaming down his lined face as the Yorkshireman retold his sad story. Because the dog had been ordered to stay, he remained in place even if that meant allowing a tractor to crush him to death. In return for the dog's remarkable loyalty, the owner could not bear to have him put down. And so he nursed him on his own kitchen table.

I have told that story to high school teenagers and asked them what they think of the dog. Most of them say, "What a stupid dog!" And they are right. It is stupid to allow yourself to be crushed out of loyalty to someone you love. But we all do it. This is foolishness as loyalty. Jesus allowed this world to crush him to death out of loyalty to God and to his people. Here is the Fool at his most powerful.

In fact, Jesus told a parable about this foolish kind of loyalty. It occurs in Luke 20:9–16, but let me paraphrase it as my own story.

Let's say that Carolyn and I own a piece of land up the coast that we can't really make much use of, so we offered it to a family who were really struggling. We helped them by putting a mobile home on the land and charging them a minimal rent. We felt good about ourselves, having been so charitable and all. But things began to awry. The tenants refused to pay the very modest rental we had set. They allowed the place to run down to the extent that the neighborhood council was complaining to us about the eyesore it was causing. Time and again we sent word to them as kindly, but firmly, as we could. We rang. We sent a local agent around. We made the trip up there several times ourselves. All to no avail.

In the end we thought that maybe our son could talk some sense into them. He was about their age. At least he had a better chance of getting through to them than we did. And so our son drove up the coast to let them know how shabbily they had been treating us, in spite of our generosity to them. When he arrived, they grabbed him and hauled him around the back of their house, tortured him, then murdered him.

When Jesus first told this story, it concerned a vineyard, not a piece of land up the coast, and he ended his parable by saying, "What will the owner of the vineyard do to them? He will come and kill those tenants and give the vineyard to others." At least that is what any human father would do. His heart would burn with rage that his tenants had not only abused his sacrificial generosity but had also destroyed his own son. Strangely, that's not what God did.

Even though we tortured and destroyed God's Son he, like the Hound of Heaven, refused to give up on us. In his steadfast loyalty, he performed two remarkable miracles. The first, as you might have imagined, is the miracle of Easter, that God raised his crucified Son from the dead. But the second miracle is sometimes even more hard to believe. Having brought him to life again, God sent his Son back to the very people who destroyed him in the first place. This is for me the most astounding evidence of the foolishness of loyalty. Even though we crucified his Son, God gave him back to us again. Not because we deserve him, but because his crazy love for us can do nothing else.

In the face of Jesus' dogged steadfastness, how could we but offer him our own loyal allegiance? As we have seen, our decision to serve Jesus should be made not in order to earn Jesus' grace but as a response to it. He who has given so much for us can rightly call us to lay down our lives for him. Recognizing that we will continue to stumble and fall short of his impeccable standard, we nonetheless strain onward out of gratitude for his mercy and kindness to us. Why do we serve the poor or preach the Gospel? Why do we continue with the otherwise foolish work of peace-making or justice-seeking? Not out of some neurotic fear of losing God's favor but precisely because we have tasted that favor and would do anything for the one who died to win it for us.

Another foolish king once asked his subjects to embrace the folly of a lost cause as Jesus does us. On St. Crispin's Day, October 25, 1415, the English and Welsh army of King Henry V lined up against the French forces under Charles VI at the Battle of Agincourt. Hopelessly outnumbered, Henry's soldiers faced a fighting force of over 36,000 Frenchmen led by battle-hardened Armagnac noblemen. Henry's British forces amounted to less than 6,000 troops. It was a desperate situation. Nearly two hundred years later William Shakespeare was to immortalize this moment in English history in his play, *Henry V.* He depicts Henry rallying his outnumbered troops with the now-famous St. Crispin's Day speech that concludes this way:

> *We few, we happy few, we band of brothers;*
> *For he today that sheds his blood with me*
> *Shall be my brother; be he ne'er so vile,*

This day shall gentle his condition;
Make him a member of the gentry, even if he is a commoner.
And gentlemen in England now a-bed
Shall think themselves accurs'd they were not here,
And hold their manhoods cheap whiles any speaks
That fought with us upon Saint Crispin's day.

History records that Henry's archers cut the French forces to ribbons with their longbows, before his foot soldiers charged into battle, humbling their enemy in one of military history's greatest upsets. Henry won at Agincourt with his vastly inferior force, his "happy few," his "band of brothers."

Today, Jesus calls us to similarly foolish loyal service when he says to us,

If any want to become my followers, let then deny themselves and take up their cross and follow me. For those who want to save their life will lose it, and those who lose their life for my sake, and for the sake of the gospel, will save it. (Mark 8:34–35)

It might make no sense to hand your life over to the un-lauded and often unappreciated work of the Gospel. With hardly any encouragement, we, Jesus' band of brothers and sisters, will press on to this foolish work of justice and mission, peace and love, mercy and hospitality. He who denied himself and was crushed for our sin has shown us the way of the cross. Today is our St. Crispin's Day. This day we face the seeming intractable forces of hostility, war, violence, poverty, and injustice, and the Fool calls us to take up the cross and to charge into action. What form this will take in your life is between you and God. But let this be known: Jesus did not die that we might just experience some personal, privatized faith that emanates in a warm, inner glow and a deep sense of well-being. He died that we might follow him loyally into battle against the forces of darkness in our world. We happy few will follow him wherever he leads.

CONCLUSION: NOT A CONCEPT BUT A NAME

A nd so we have come to the end of the road. Luke has led us from Jesus' break with the prophetic style of John the Baptist along the rocky path to Jerusalem and his ultimate destruction and final victory. As we have traveled, we have had our eyes opened to new ways of seeing ourselves, our God and each other. And we have been overwhelmed by the devotion that took Jesus to Gethsemane and then to the cross.

It is a unique and difficult journey, this journey of faith in Jesus. It takes hard work and plenty of courage. But I assure you it is a trip worth taking.

Indeed, it has become a journey for me that so totally defines my sense of reality and my own self-understanding that I can't imagine not being on this road. I am reminded of the poignant words of the great Swiss theologian, Karl Barth. Whatever one might think of Barth's theology, you cannot but admire his great, lifelong devotion to Jesus, a journey that survived the ravages of Nazism and the aftermath of the Holocaust. In 1968, during the last year of his life at the age of 82, he wrote the following:

> The last word I have to say . . . is not a concept like grace but a name: Jesus Christ. He is grace and he is the ultimate one beyond world and church and even theology. We cannot lay hold of him. But we have to do with him. And my own concern in my long life has been

increasingly to emphasize this name and to say, "In him." There is no salvation but in this name. In him is grace.[38]

His final word was not a theological concept, although he was regarded as one of the twentieth century's greatest theologians. His final word is a name. The name of Jesus. It is Jesus, Barth concludes, that we cannot lay hold of but that we must ultimately have to do with. It is the Jesus of grace, of salvation, of forgiveness that we should emphasize to our dying breath.

Barth signs off this note with the following: "In him is all that I have attempted in my life in weakness and folly. It is there in him."[39] Surely, this should be our testimony as well: that all we have attempted, whether in weakness or in folly (or both) is done "in him," as a response to his foolish wisdom, his foolish grace, his foolish sacrifice. I close this small book with the confession that all I have attempted has been both weakness and folly, but that at the core it has been an attempt to respond to the grace offered freely by Jesus. Like Barth, then, I end not with a concept, but a name.

Jesus.

ENDNOTES

1. M. Scott Peck, *Further Along the Road Less Traveled* (New York: Simon and Schuster, 1993), 210.

2. Alastair V. Campbell, *Rediscovering Pastoral Care* (Philadelphia: Westminster, 1981), 50.

3. In Harvey Cox, *The Feast of Fools* (Cambridge: Harvard University Press, 1969).

4. 2 Samuel 11:1.

5. 2 Samuel 12:1–4.

6. Jonah 1:1, 2.

7. Jonah 1:3.

8. Campbell, 1981, 51.

9. Richard Bandler and John Grinder, *Reframing: Neuro-Linguistic Programming and the Transformation of Meaning* (Moab, Utah: Real People Press, 1982), 1.

10. Bandler and Grinder, 1982, 9.

11. Romans 6:1–2a.

12. C. S. Lewis, *Mere Christianity* (New York: Macmillan, 1952), 55.

13. Philip Dormer Stanhope, 4th Earl Chesterfield, *Letters Written by the Late Right Honourable Philip Dormer Stanhope, 4th Earl, Earl of Chesterfield, to his Son* (5th ed.; vol. II; London, 1774), 21.

14. Luci Shaw, "It is as if infancy were the whole of incarnation," in *Polishing the Petoskey Stone* (Carol Stream, Ill.: Harold Shaw, 1990). I encourage you to find and read the entire poem.

15. John Donne, *Devotions upon Emergent Occasions,* no. 17, 108–9 (1959). Originally published in 1624.

16. Malcom X, speech, December 12, 1963, New York City, posted at www.bartlebys.com.

17. Kenneth Bailey, *Through Peasant Eyes* (Grand Rapids: Eerdmans, 1980), 71–73.

18. Kenneth Bailey, *Poet and Peasant* (Grand Rapids: Eerdmans, 1976), 99, quoting Asher Feldman, *The Parables and Similes of the Rabbis* (Cambridge: Cambridge University Press, 1924), 239.

19. Bailey, 1976, 100.

20. Jacques Ellul, *Money and Power* (Downer's Grove, Ill.: InterVarsity, 1984), 109.

21. Ellul, 1984, 110.

22. Ellul, 1984, 133.

23. Ash Barker, *Make Poverty Personal: the Bible's Call to End Oppression* (Melbourne: UNOH, 2006), 103.

24. Ellul, 1984, 150.

25. Barker, 2006, 103–4.

26. Henri J. M. Nouwen, *Reaching Out* (Glasgow: Collins, 1976), 68–69.

27. Nouwen, 1976, 95.

28. Phyllis Theroux, *New York Times*, 17 July 1980.

29. Michka Assayas, *Bono: in Conversation with Michka Assayas* (New York: Riverhead, 2005), 134.

30. C. S. Lewis, *Surprised by Joy* (London: Geoffrey Bles, 1955), 211–12.

31. Matthew 16:16.

32. Matthew 16:22.

33. In *God: What the Critics Say*, ed. Martin Wroe (London: Spire, 1992), 31.

34. Tracy Chapman, in "Matters of the Heart," EMI Songs, 1992, from the album *Matter of the Heart*, Elektra.

35. Quoted in Morton T. Kelsey, *Caring* (New York: Paulist, 1981), 26–27.

36. Campbell, 1981, 53.

37. Matthew 26:36–46.

38. Karl Barth, *A Karl Barth Reader* (ed. Rolf Joachim Erler and Reiner Marquard; Grand Rapids: Eerdmans, 1986), 114.

39. Ibid.